THE LITTLE HISTORY OF BIRMINGHAM

VANESSA MORGAN

The History Press

First published 2025

The History Press
97 St George's Place, Cheltenham,
Gloucestershire, GL50 3QB
www.thehistorypress.co.uk

British Library Cataloguing in Publication Data.
A catalogue record for this book is available from the British Library.

ISBN 978 1 80399 858 9

Typesetting and origination by The History Press.
Printed and bound in Great Britain by TJ Books Limited, Padstow, Cornwall.

MIX
Paper | Supporting responsible forestry
FSC® C013056
FSC www.fsc.org

Trees for Life

CONTENTS

AUTHOR'S FOREWORD

Vanessa Morgan was born just over the border in Worcestershire, but her mother and grandmother were true Brummies. This meant regular visits to family and shopping trips into town. Working life took her into Birmingham. As a genealogist, many hours were spent in Birmingham Library or on visits to locations connected to a family she was researching. And as a TV extra, Vanessa worked on location in the city on such programmes as *Doctors* and the popular children's programme, lovingly entitled *Brum*.

Birmingham took root as a small Saxon community, but today it spreads across an extremely large area. So, for the purposes of this book, the story being told is of the whole of this large district, including all the suburbs of Birmingham that were once towns and villages in their own right, but now form part of the metropolis still lovingly known as Brum.

There are many stories in this little book that, it is hoped, will install a desire in the reader to further explore the bits that grab their interest.

FROM FOREST TO MARKET TOWN

Imagine a large, shallow lake surrounded by hills and rocky slopes in a climate hotter than it is today with no sign of life. Is this a scene from a sci-fi film? No, it is Birmingham millions of years ago. On the bed of this lake there was a thick layer of mud that had been formed from silt rolling down from the rocky crevices in the hills. This mud became known as Mercia mudstone. When the climate changed, the lake dried up and the clay cracked. These cracks would eventually become the rivers Rea, Tame and Cole.

Then came the Ice Age, and Birmingham, together with much of what became Great Britain, was buried beneath 3,000m of ice. Glaciers slowly moved across the whole area, moving masses of stones and earth across the land. When the great thaw came, once again the landscape changed. Boulders, stones and pebbles were left strewn across the country and the cracks in the dried-up lakes were filled with gushing water. Vegetation began to grow, and the Forest of Arden was formed.

AN OLD ROCKY REMINDER

One of these stones from the Ice Age can be found in Key Hill Cemetery. It is a volcanic rock that, after a study made by scientists, is thought to have originally come from the mountains of Wales and was carried to Birmingham by glaciers. As the ice melted it was left behind.

It became known as the Hoar Stone, which in old English is '*har stan field*', meaning 'boundary stone in a field', and was used as a marker for the boundaries of the Birmingham, Aston and Handsworth manors in earlier times. Now swallowed up by modern-day development, it stands on a plinth, as a memorial to an age long gone. An inscription reads, 'This felsite boulder was deposited near here by a glacier during the Ice Age being at one time used as a parish boundary mark, it was known as the Hoare Stone of which the modern War Stone is a corruption.'

It was from this that Warstone Lane was derived.

Other such boulders that were brought down from north Wales by glaciers can be found lying around Birmingham. One sits in Cannon Hill Park. Known as 'the Boulder', it sits by the boating lake and has stood there since the park was opened. Another can be found in Olton Park. Two others have also given names to where they sat – for example, the Great Stone Inn in Northfield and Gilberstone Avenue, Yardley.

PREHISTORIC BRUMMIES

When early humans arrived in Birmingham, they found an area of variety – patchy woodland, stony heaths, brooks trickling from springs in the clay crevices and other parts that were boggy and difficult to traverse. But they left behind some of their tools to reveal their presence, and although only a few Stone Age tools have been found, it is enough evidence to prove there was a small population here. These nomads, who didn't settle in any particular place but travelled around as hunters and gatherers, left behind a man-made axe in a garden in Court Lane, Erdington, a type of scraper in Northfield and other bits and pieces in Saltley. Tools specific to the Bronze Age were found under Mackadown Farm when it was demolished in the 1950s.

Gradually, these tribes became more settled. They wanted to build homes for themselves where they could live permanently. In some parts of Birmingham, they found the soil was too light to farm and didn't drain sufficiently. However, there were parts that consisted of clay, and although difficult for a farmer to plough, it did make good pots. But in the parts where the glaciers had moved numerous amounts of sand and gravel, the land was drier and easier to plough, and this is where the first Brummies built their settlements.

THE IRON AGE BRUMMIE

Around 600 BC, we were in the Iron Age. Humans had learned how to smelt iron using charcoal and could make tools and weapons. Living in larger communities of sometimes up to 1,000, they built wooden circular huts with wattle and daub and thatched, pointed roofs. They bred sheep, cows and pigs and grew crops. Their villages would be enclosed by moats and fences.

As they became more territorial, they became warriors and built hill forts as protection for their communities. The nearest known hill fort to Birmingham is at Shirley and is known as Berry Mound. It covers around 12 acres, and although it has never been excavated and was subjected to constant agriculture in the nineteenth century, a bank and ditch give a very clear view of its size.

Other evidence of Iron Age humans found in the Birmingham area include a glass bead found in a park in Castle Bromwich and some fragments of pottery from Selly Oak. However, the biggest find was during excavations prior to the M6 Toll being built. On the east side of Solihull, evidence of a moat was found together with the foundations of some circular huts.

There were three known tribal districts around Birmingham. In the south were the Dobunni, whose capital was in Cirencester. Using the River Cole as their boundary were the Cornovii and the Corieltauvi. The Cornovii came from the Wrekin, where it is thought their capital was, and spread out to the west of Birmingham. The Corieltauvi, whose capital was in Leicester, could be found in the east.

INVASION

So, by the first century, the people of Birmingham – and Britain – had become more organised, living in their tribes and led by individual kings and queens. However, they were not as powerful nor as civilised as the people from a then faraway land who were rapidly building a large empire.

The Romans first arrived on the Kent coast in AD 43, and although records are very sketchy, it is thought there were probably around four legions of Roman soldiers together with a cavalry of auxiliary troops. This would possibly make a total of 40,000 men. The campaign was long, and it took around forty years for the Romans to take complete control of the majority of England and Wales.

Birmingham was only on the edge of the Roman occupation, perhaps due to it being a dense forest area in the east, with the ground to the west not being suitable for agriculture. The only current evidence of a Roman existence here is the fort at Metchley and Icknield Street, the Roman road, although archaeological surveys do suggest there may have been a Roman farm at King's Norton and that pottery was made in the Witton area. And when ground was being excavated for the Bull Ring, there was evidence of a farm once being there and it was thought it could be Roman.

But there is evidence that battles took place here, presumably with the tribes mentioned previously. When ground was being levelled for the building of the canals in the late 1700s and early 1800s, many pieces of ancient items were found. These included swords, battleaxes and buckles, although they were never confirmed to be Roman or otherwise.

All Roads Lead to Rome

As the Romans progressed through the country, they began building their roads, something for which history has credited them with glowing reports. Ryknield Street, also known as Icknield Street, ran between Southampton and Tynemouth and entered Birmingham in the south-west along the Pershore Road, Bournville Lane to Harborne and then Warstone Lane. Crossing Hockley Brook, it headed out towards Sutton Coldfield. Although the original cannot be seen in Birmingham, in the 1800s a stretch of it was still very much visible in Sutton Park. A writer in the early 1800s said that parts of it in Sutton Park and on the Coldfield were in perfect repair 'as when the Romans left it'.

The Roman Brummie

Metchley Fort was situated near Harborne and was always thought to have been built by the Romans, but some historians have disagreed with this. Some believe it was built by the Danes, although there is no evidence of the Danes ever being here; others feel that it was built by the ancient Britons to ward off the arrival of the Romans. There is also a conflict as to how big it was. In the 1700s writers were suggesting it covered an area of 30 acres, but when it was measured in 1822 it only appeared to be 15 acres.

The camp was named Bremenium. Translated, '*Bre*' and '*Maen*' mean high stone. Certainly, where the fort had been built, the Romans would have got a good view of the surrounding country and being built close to Icknield Street meant an easy journey to another camp at Wall, near Lichfield, and then on to Watling Street.

ANOTHER INVASION

Finding it difficult to defend themselves against the Germanic tribes now attacking the British coast, and with trouble brewing in other parts of their empire, the Romans left in the early fifth century. Coming from northern Europe, Germany and Scandinavia, these Germanic tribes were divided into two groups, the Saxons and the Vikings, and they quickly populated Britain. There is no evidence that the Vikings ever came to Birmingham, although they must have passed by when travelling to Shropshire, possibly using the old Watling Street, which lay to the north of Birmingham. But the Saxons quickly inhabited the area and so Birmingham was born.

THE NEW BRUMMIE

A tribe known as the Hwicca spread across England from the south-west through Worcestershire and Warwickshire, but the Forest of Arden prevented them reaching Birmingham before another Saxon party did. This tribe had arrived at the mouth of the River Trent in Humberside and had travelled across country following the Trent and then the River Tame before pushing their way through the forest. Here a group settled on the banks of the River Rea, near to where Gooch Street is today. They were the Ingas of Beorma, in other words, the Beorma family, and as Saxon settlements were called *hams*, this has always been considered the way Birmingham got its name. However, another suggestion by historian William Hutton refers to the name Bromych, which eventually became Bromycham, taken from broom (a shrub growing in the area) and *wych* (meaning descent).

Another tribe settled at Edbald's Tom (Edgbaston) and one at East Town (Aston). Other settlements developed in the surrounding areas of heathland, and they were to become known as King's Heath, Small Heath and Balsall Heath.

Later, all these tribes merged into one and then this part of middle England became the Kingdom of Mercia.

Birmingham Names

Soon Birmingham was covered in other small hamlets with names reflecting what or who could be found there. In some cases, their modern names were derived from those Anglo-Saxon names.

Dudd – Duddeston
Deritend – Der-yat-end or Dear Gate End
Digbeth – Dyke Path or Ducks' Bath
Stirchley – road clearing
Mackadown – Macca's farm. Also known as Machitone
Yardley – farm clearing in dense oak forest (and also known as the spot where a missionary came to preach to a Saxon community)
Northfield – land already cleared
Saltley – willow for basket weaving
Ashold – ash trees
Bromford – good river crossing
Stetchford – not a good river crossing
Greet Hill – passable all the time
Solihull – not accessible in winter

As these settlements grew so did the manorial system whereby lords of the manor governed lands and estates of different wealth and sizes. This was a system that continued for hundreds of years with a king or queen at the head. The Saxons and the ancient Britons soon became one and so the Anglo-Saxon era began.

Hundreds

Introduced around 613 as part of the plan to divide the country up into shires and counties, the hundreds also meant there was a regular court system, with each hundred having its own court and officers. There was no courthouse to begin with, and the hundred court was held at an ancient site, such as a stone, tree or crossroads, before purpose-built buildings were erected.

Birmingham belonged to the Hemlingford hundred and lay in the west of the area. It was named after the ford across the River Tame in Kingsbury, a town in Warwickshire about 10 miles north-east of Birmingham. Also including Tamworth in the north, Nuneaton in the east and Solihull in the south, the Hemlingford court was thought to have been held at crossroads in Coleshill.

A RESTING SAINT

Lying in St Chad's Roman Catholic Cathedral in Birmingham is an adopted Brummie. St Chad was the fifth Bishop of Mercia and from 669 until his death in 672, he lived in Nether Stowe, Lichfield. It was he who helped convert the Celtic pagan worshippers to Christian beliefs and he became known as the Apostle of the Midlands. When Lichfield Cathedral was built, his tomb was moved from Nether Stowe to the cathedral but when civil war broke out, it was taken away and hidden from the Puritans. He then found his way to Birmingham.

An area known as Chad Valley, north of Harborne and Edgbaston, was thought to have been named after him, but it could also have derived from the name Shadwell, meaning shallow boundary brook, as a brook does run through the area. Now known as Chad Brook, it joins the Bourn Brook before running into the River Rea.

DOMESDAY AND THE HANDING OUT OF LAND

Leading up to the end of the Anglo-Saxon era, the manor of Birmingham belonged to Ulwine, also known as Alwyne, the son of Wigod the Dane, who had married the sister of Leofric, the Saxon Earl of Mercia, therefore uniting the two civilisations. But now another invader arrived from Normandy and more changes took place.

Following the Norman Conquest in 1066, the manors of Birmingham, Edgbaston, Selly Oak, Northfield, Aston, Erdington, Witton, Handsworth, Perry and Little Barr were all given to Ansculf de Picquigny and then passed to his son, William Fitz-Ansculf. They had come over with William the Conqueror from Picquigny in the Somme but made their home at the Saxon castle in Dudley.

William Fitz-Ansculf had just one daughter, Beatrix, who married Fulke de Paynel. When her father died, these manors became the property of the Paynel family, but by the twelfth century and into the early thirteenth century, they had been split up between other families such as the de Berminghams, the atte Holtes, the de Erdingtons and the de Somery family.

The Domesday Survey shows that Birmingham contained four hides, with half an acre of wood, which was half a mile long and 4 furlongs in breadth, and enough land for six ploughs. It was worth 20 shillings. There were nine residents made up of five villeins (villagers who farmed several strips of land) and four borders (villagers who farmed a very small plot of land) with two ploughs.

Aston consisted of eight hides, a church, mill and woodland. With five times the population, it was worth £5. The overlord here was simply known as Godmund.

Edgbaston, known as Celboldstone, had two hides and half a mile of wood. The ten residents were ruled by Drogo. He was a Norman soldier who had fought with Ansculf.

Erdington had nine villeins, three smallholders and two slaves. There were 5 acres of meadow, six plough fields and woodland all worth £1 10*s*, plus a mill worth 3 shillings.

In Selly Oak there were seven villeins and sixteen smallholders with six cottages, three slaves, one priest, nineteen ploughlands and one woodland. It was worth £5.

Witton had just one villein, two smallholders and two slaves. There were four plough lands, and it was worth £1.

Handsworth just consisted of two plough lands with 2 acres of meadow and a mill. It was worth 2 shillings.

Perry and Little Barr were just listed as an abandoned settlement.

A Family Takes Charge of its Lands

Sometime in the mid-twelfth century, the de Bermingham family acquired the manor of Birmingham from the Paynell family, also known as Paganell. Peter de Bermingham applied to Henry II in 1154 for a market charter for the purpose of selling livestock. The date may not be entirely accurate and some historians say it was 1166, but it was granted. Records show that at some time Peter was listed as a steward to Gervaise Paganell.

The Bermingham family are thought to have originated from Picquigny, and Richard, who fought with Ansculf, was rewarded with land in Birmingham. Richard had a son, William, who not a lot is known about, and it was his son Peter who adopted the name de Bermingham. The Paganell family had become Barons of Dudley, and it seems Peter served them well and was rewarded with more land and was made Gervaise Paganell's chief steward and second in command.

With his newly acquired grandeur, Peter built himself a moated manor house. The Moat, as the house was called, was about 8 yards south of St Martin's Church and replaced a castle that had been built around 1140. It is not clear what had happened to the castle, whether Peter demolished it to build his new manor house or if it had been destroyed by King Stephen during his war with Matilda. However, there is no evidence that Stephen was ever in the area.

There are believed to have been three royal visits to the de Bermingham family: one from King Richard I in 1189 and two for King John in 1206 and 1208.

A TOWN QUIETLY GROWS

Birmingham avoided getting involved in any of the wars and skirmishes that blew up at various times in the history of England – the conflict between Stephen and Matilda and the Wars of the Roses, for example. On the whole, Birmingham and its families sat out these events as the town quietly grew.

In 1181 there were eighteen freeholders cultivating 667 acres with thirty-five tenants holding 158 acres. The total value was £13 8*s* 2*d*.

One of the oldest streets in Birmingham is Edgbaston Street. Originally, it was the road that led from St Martin's and the manor house to Edgbaston and was used by the de Birmingham family to visit their neighbours in Edgbaston. Known in King John's reign as 'Egebaston Strete', strete being the word used to describe a paved way in cities and towns, it was the first street in the town to be paved.

There was a mill in the Moor Street area called the Town Mill. The miller was called John le Moul or le Molendin. Through various phonetic variations of the name, the street on which he lived became known as Moor Street. Together with Edgbaston Street, this is said to be the oldest in Birmingham, and is probably older than Edgbaston Street. There was at one time a wooden bridge over a stream that crossed the street. It became the street where many of the old Birmingham families resided – Carless, Smallbroke, Ward, Sheldon, Flavell and Stidman, among others, who all paid rent to the lord of the manor.

A NEW DAWN FOR BIRMINGHAM

In the 1300s, the town was mainly filled with timber-framed buildings known as cruck houses and its market was a thriving place to be. These were typical of many houses throughout the country and were basic homes with one large lower room with a hearth, and at the other end steps led to a smaller upper room. One typical cruck house was Minworth Greaves, which was built on the outskirts of Sutton Coldfield. Rescued from demolition in the early 1900s by George Cadbury, it was rebuilt at his newly developed Bournville and is still on view there today.

A typical Cruck House, still found in modern country villages.

Improvements began to take place, and in 1319 a three-year patent was taken out to improve the roads in Birmingham. The finances didn't stretch to completing the task, so in 1333 a second patent was taken out and tolls were fixed at 1 farthing for every 8 bushels of corn. Apparently though, as later stories tell, the slabs were placed the wrong way up and therefore the surface was uneven and painful to the feet. How long these slabs lasted is not recorded, but when these roads were paved in 1819 the system had improved. A steam-paving engine did the job this time. With its six heavy hammers, it easily drove any uneven stones into the roads as the engine slowly moved about 1ft at a time.

In a document dated 1347, Lady Well is listed as a 'dwelling in Edgbaston Street leading towards God Well Field'. The well had been dedicated to the Virgin Mary and was close to the house, which was later known as the Parsonage or Rectory, where priests found shelter. The spring was very abundant and filled the moat around the Parsonage. From there it was joined by waters from the hill at Holloway Head and went via Edgbaston Street to fill the moat around the Manor House.

The Chester Road, a busy road today, was also an important highway in these times. The Earl of Warwick, who was Lord of Sutton manor, built a cottage to house two men who assisted travellers across Sutton Chase, a desolate area that was well known for harbouring bandits. Known as Bow Bearers Lodge, it existed right up to the early 1800s when it was demolished. The empty field became known as Bow Bearers Croft and is now immortalised as Bowcroft Grove.

A STRING OF WILLIAMS

In 1252, a charter for holding a fair was given to William de Bermingham by Henry III. The fair was held at Whitsun and Michaelmas.

William, who had inherited the manor in 1246, was the grandson of Peter de Bermingham and his father had also been named William. He married the daughter of Thomas of Astley and joined his father-in-law in the Barons' War. He was killed in the Battle of Evesham in 1265. Because of his involvement in the uprising, his lands, which were then valued at £40, were confiscated and given to Roger de Clifford. However, they were returned to the family when his son, William the third, paid a fine. This William, as a military knight, joined Edward I during the Gascon Campaign and while attempting to relieve the Fortress of Bonnegarde was captured, along with other knights, and taken to Paris. He did make it back to Birmingham and survived until 1306, when the fourth William inherited.

The fifth and last William helped raise troops, 400 in total, for Edward III in 1326 and for this he was given the title Lord William de Bermingham. He became a Member of Parliament, but the succession of Williams ended with him. His son was Sir Fouke de Bermingham, who succeeded around 1340 and followed his father into Parliament as MP for Warwick.

The last of the de Bermingham family, Edward, was born in 1497 and succeeded his grandfather when he was only 3 years old. And it was this that eventually resulted in the demise of the Bermingham family – a story that will be told later.

THE PARISH CHURCH

In the late thirteenth century, a new church was built to replace an earlier Norman one. Since then, St Martin's has seen many improvements. In 1690 it was encased in red brick, apart from the spire, which provided a cover for the original sandstone as it was beginning to show wear and tear. Between 1873 and 1875 it was again completely rebuilt, the idea being to return it back to the Gothic appearance it would have had when first built. Further restoration was necessary after damage caused by the bombings of the Second World War.

However, in all this time four stone figures survived. It is highly likely they are members of the Bermingham family, with one being the William de Bermingham who fought in the French Wars with Edward I. But of the other three, it is not certain who is who. William carries the distinctive shield showing the diagonal line from upper right to lower left, with five lozenges, which has always been incorporated in the city arms.

In 1330 and 1347, father and son Walter of Clodeshale and Richard of Clodeshale endowed a 'chauntry' in St Martin's for their daily use and that of their families and descendants. Walter was a wealthy and influential wool merchant from Birmingham and in 1343 bought the manor of Saltley.

NEIGHBOURHOOD DISPUTE

The manor of King's Norton was owned by the king and within it was an area known as Kingswood. Roger Mortimer, Earl of March, who already had several possessions, was given the manor of King's Norton by Edward II in 1317. Around seven years later, Roger had a ditch dug, almost a mile in length, to enclose his land in Kingswood, which up until then had been common land within the parishes of Kings Norton, Yardley and Solihull.

His neighbours were not happy and demolished it, with the bailiff getting killed during the scuffle. It must have been considered an accident because Mortimer only charged them with trespass. He did win and was awarded £300 damages. However, Mortimer was a ruthless man at court and was involved in many intrigues and made several enemies. He was eventually arrested and executed. After his execution his neighbours petitioned Edward III, who reduced the fine to £40. The area is now known as Druids Heath.

THE HOLTE FAMILY OF ASTON

The Holte family are of Saxon origin, their name meaning grove or woody place, and they became wealthy exporting wool across Europe in vast quantities. Their connections with Aston began around 1331 when Simon Holte bought the manor of Nechells from the widow of Sir George de Castells, followed in 1363 when John Holte bought the manor of Duddeston and two years later, the Manor of Aston. Their place of residence was then Duddeston Hall.

In 1400 William Holte gathered 120 men to take supplies of herring and flour from London to Scotland by ship to Henry IV's army. This luckily put him in the king's debt and when four years later, the manor was taken by the local escheator following the Act of Resumption, William had no problem in having the manor returned to him.

In March 1406, he was once again coming to the aid of the king when he accompanied the king's son, Thomas of Lancaster, to Ireland. His favour with the royal family continued into the reign of Henry V and by 1419 he had become a friend of the Earl of Warwick, who he accompanied to France. In 1422, the earl gave him the post of Sheriff of Worcestershire. He died around 1435/36 and his nephew, John Holte, succeeded him.

The Holts were to become a prestigious family in Aston. By the 1500s, Thomas Holt was a Justice for north Wales and his marriage to Marjorie Winnington had brought the family more land and wealth. When he died in 1545, his estate was valued at £270 *6s 2d* and showed that his residence had thirteen bedrooms and ten other rooms with a couple of smaller rooms adjoining those. It was described as containing 'splendid hangings' of blues and reds.

THE OLDE CROWN INN

In 1368, the Old Crown Inn was built in Deritend, and it is still standing in the same place at No. 188 High Street. It wasn't originally an inn. In 1538 it is simply described as a 'mansion house of tymber'. Parts of the original building are still there, although the majority dates to the early 1500s. It survived Prince Rupert's attack on the area during the Civil War, Hitler's bombs and more modern redevelopment plans in the district. One historian wrote in the late 1800s that, at that time, it had been owned by the same family, the Smiths, for many years.

Queen Elizabeth I is supposed to have stayed there for one night on her way back to London from Kenilworth Castle. She slept in a room above the main entrance.

The earliest record of it being described as an inn was in 1626 and it was only from 1666 that it was known as the Crown. However, in 1684 it once again became a dwelling house and was converted into two cottages; then in 1693, into three cottages. It wasn't until the end of the nineteenth century that it once again became an inn.

The Olde Crown.

At the back of the property there is a courtyard and here can be found a well that is thought to have been sunk 1,000 years ago.

In 1851 the inn was in peril of being demolished as part of the Birmingham Corporation's plans for improving the area, but lawyer Joshua Toulmin Smith rescued it. It was in peril again in 1856 and 1862, but once again Smith managed to get the Corporation to change their plans and in 1863 he repaired the well and added iron railings. In the 1880s the well began to suffer neglect and lay forgotten until 1994, when new owners took over and it was discovered hidden among the old sheds.

Another pub over in Erdington often causes debates as to whether it is the oldest pub in Birmingham. The Lad in the Lane, previously known as the Old Green Man, sits on the Bromford Road and certainly has bits of its building work that do date back to the fourteenth century. It too started as an ordinary house before becoming Ye Olde Green Man in the 1780s.

A DAMSEL IN DISTRESS

The Middlemore family's connection with Edgbaston began in the 1390s when Thomas Middlemore became attracted to Isabel, the heiress of Sir Richard de Edgbaston. Sometime around 1395, Sir Richard was away fighting and Isabel was left alone. Middlemore decided to take advantage of this situation and rode to Edgbaston to court her. He found her being attacked in the woods around Edgbaston Hall by thieves. After rescuing her, she was soon his, and their descendants remained in Edgbaston for the next 300 years. They also helped finance the ships that fought the Spanish Armada in 1588.

WEOLEY CASTLE

Weoley was a Saxon settlement, the name meaning temple clearing, and evidence shows there was probably an early earthwork there before a wooden building was built on top of it. This building was burned down sometime in the thirteenth century and a stone castle with six towers built around the time of the Barons' War.

Roger de Somery owned the Manor of Weoley and fought for the king in the Barons' War. At the time, as was the fashion, many landed gentry were crenelating their manor houses and having to pay the king for a licence to do so. However, it is thought that as a reward Roger was given his licence for free.

By 1273 the surrounding park was well stocked with deer, and over the next 200 years the castle was altered and rebuilt several times. In 1495, it was owned by Sir William Berkeley, who was a supporter of Richard III and the York side, so when Henry VII became king the Berkeley estates were forfeited and given to his uncle, Jasper Tudor, Duke of Bedford. It seems Jasper wasn't interested in the estate because within ten days he had sold it to Lord John Dudley.

Ten years later Jasper died, and the king decided to take possession of the estate. After Sir William Berkeley died in 1501, he granted the manor to William's son, Richard Berkley, who was also lord of the manor of Northfield.

Around 1523, the castle and grounds were sold to a wealthy London mercer called Richard Jervoise and his family remained in possession of the estate for the next 300 years. But the castle was never occupied and by the seventeenth century it was in ruins.

CHANGES IN THE 1500S

Birmingham was surrounded by many other manors and parishes – Handsworth, the hamlet of Perry Barr, Aston, Water Orton, Erdington, Bordesley, Saltley, Duddeston and Nechells, Yardley, King's Norton, Northfield and Harborne – and by the 1500s, it and many of these neighbouring parishes were showing their industrial future. As well as being home to fulling mills for cleansing cloth and corn mills for flour, the River Rea was now also home to blade mills for grinding the edges of tools.

There were tanneries for the making of leather, which were mostly situated around Edgbaston Street, and manorial records show that the town had two leather-sealers whose job it was to ensure that the leather supplied to the markets was of good quality. Digbeth was also home to around a dozen tanning yards and this area became known as Tanner's Row. It was certainly a good area for the tanners as it was close to the oak barks of the Forest of Arden and the waters of the River Rea. However, Tanner's Row was very close to the manor house, and it is for this reason, it is believed, that the de Bermingham family moved out. The smell from the tanneries could be quite pungent.

Being a mill owner at that time must have been a prestigious occupation because one appears to have been wealthy enough to attract the attentions of Edward de Bermingham's widow. William Ascrick became the third husband of Elizabeth de Bermingham.

In Tudor times, St Martin's was a busy area containing clusters of shops and houses. The narrow street at the west end of the church was known as Mercer Street, where a growing cloth trade could be found. At the east end of the church was Well Street, which ran into Corn Cheaping, the location for butchers that extended into the Bull Ring. The entrance to New Street was through an arched gateway, where the Free Grammar School was situated. From there, at the junction of High Street and New Street could be found the Cross.

The Cross, sometimes called the Market Cross, was a square building that stood on top of archways. Underneath was an empty space where country folk, mainly women, brought their dairy produce and eggs to sell on market days. Above was the Toll House, where the Court Leet was held. The leather sealers also operated from here, so it became known as the Leather Hall. Market Cross was demolished when the area around St Martin's was cleared in the 1700s.

There was a similar building in Dale End named the Welsh Cross, which was demolished in 1803 and at the time, its three-dial clock and weathervane were advertised for sale. Dale End was once known as Welsh End because it was inhabited by quite a large Welsh community.

The Bull Ring was always a popular place through the centuries.

There was a gaol in Bordesley that was described as just two cellars and was situated behind the Brown Lion Inn. The gaoler was a W.D. Brownell, so the gaol became known as Brownell's Hole. His wife, Jemima, ran the inn.

In 1538 Birmingham had 1,500 inhabitants living in 200 houses on six streets. They mainly worked as smiths, making knives and other types of cutlery. Others made small iron items such as spurs and stirrups. There were also nailers, and by the end of the 1500s slitting mills had begun to appear, which divided iron bars into rods.

LOCAL BOY DOES GOOD

John Harman was born in Sutton around 1462, the son of William Harman, a farmer described as being in the lower ranks of the country gentry. Educated at Magdalen College, Oxford, John became close friends with Thomas Wolsey, later Cardinal Wolsey, and by 1489 he was a member of the household of Elizabeth of York. He became Bishop of Exeter in 1519, a post he kept until 1551, and at some time he adopted the name Vesey. His friendship with Wolsey made him popular with Henry VIII and as well as attending meetings with the king as one of his advisors, he was also tutor to the king's daughter, Princess Mary. Not being in total agreement with Henry regarding the new Church of England, his position became precarious, but he managed to keep his head.

He never forgot his home town. He obtained a charter that gave Sutton the title of royal town and he persuaded Henry to donate his hunting ground there – this became Sutton Park. Bishop Vesey also helped finance the work that saw the town paved and the church repaired. He then had fifty-one cottages built for the poor. In 1551, he retired to Moor Hall in Sutton, close to the farm where he had been born and which he had built in 1527. He died there in 1554. In his days of favour, he had entertained Henry VIII there and employed over 100 servants, all dressed in red livery.

The hall was demolished in 1903 by its owner Colonel Edward Ansell, of the brewery, in favour of a completely new building that in 1905 became a hotel – and is still a hotel today – with a golf course in the grounds.

Bishop Vesey left another legacy that is still part of the Sutton Coldfield of today – the Bishop Vesey's Grammar School. Founded in 1527, it was built on Blind Lane, Sutton, near Holy Trinity Church, but moved in 1729 to Lichfield Road where it stands today. The school's popularity dropped in the early 1800s as it continued to teach the old classical curriculum rather than the new curriculum of mathematics, English and modern languages, and by 1840 it just had one pupil. The Grammar School Act made it law for the new curriculum to be taught in all schools, so by 1866 there were fifty-one pupils and in 1875, 105.

TIME OF TROUBLE AND CHANGE

By 1530, the country was in turmoil. Henry VIII had grown tired of his wife Catherine of Aragon, and was looking for a new queen to give him a son and heir. For England, everything changed in the 1530s and Birmingham was no exception.

Henry VIII broke away from Rome and formed his own Church, then he destroyed and looted religious houses, monasteries and abbeys, keeping the estates previously owned by the Church for himself. He divorced Catherine and married Anne Boleyn, but as a parting gift to Catherine he gave her the manor of Yardley.

One local casualty of the Dissolution was Humphrey Middlemore, the son of Richard Middlemore of Edgbaston, who was a member of the Carthusian Order of the Charterhouse in London. In 1534, Henry VIII insisted that prominent members of the Church should acknowledge his marriage to

Anne Boleyn. The Royal Commissioners visited Charterhouse so that the monks could take the oath. Humphrey, among others, refused. They spent a month in the tower but were then released. A year later, they refused to sign the Oath of Supremacy, and although some who refused were sent to Tyburn to be executed, Humphrey again survived. However, a month later he wasn't so lucky. On 19 June 1535, Thomas Cromwell drew up a warrant for his arrest and he was executed at Tyburn.

LOSSES AND GAINS

The Priory (also known as Hospital) of St Thomas the Apostle would have been situated somewhere at the top of Corporation Street across to Dale End. Records show it was built around 1285 when William de Bermingham, Thomas of Maidenhacche and Ranulph of Rugby gave 23 acres of ground in Birmingham and Aston for the erection of the hospital. However, it is thought that there was a religious building already there. The de Bermingham family gave another 22 acres in 1320. Later, in 1350, another 70 acres were given in Birmingham, and 30 acres in Aston. After the Dissolution, the majority of these lands went to the Holte family, while the immediate grounds surrounding the priory and chapel were sold in various lots, with the Smallbroke family purchasing the majority of this.

The Smallbrokes had originated from Yardley, where they had been recorded as yeomen as far back as the twelfth century. They still owned land in Yardley. Richard Smallbroke was born in 1515 and became wealthy selling cloth, spices and groceries, as well as being involved in the iron trade. He is recorded as living in Park Street. The years following the Dissolution saw the family soar to greater heights and his son, Richard, became so wealthy that in 1590 he built the splendid Blakesley Hall – an extremely modern house for the period with large fireplaces and glass in its windows.

As far as the priory was concerned, by the eighteenth century there was nothing left of the buildings. The stones had been used across the town for building.

The Colmore family originated from Tournai in Belgium and had made their wealth in the cloth industry, but also in land investments. William Colmore, a mercer at No. 1 High Street, bought the Conyngre (the rabbit warren) of St Thomas' Priory, which had been used to breed rabbits for food and fur. He later went on to finance forty-three ships, which sailed out to stop the Spanish Armada.

The family also owned the Bell Barn Estate and in the early 1600s, his son, William, built New Hall, a large mansion house to the north of what is now Colmore Row and which is now known as Newhall Street. During the Civil War they were a Parliamentarian family and one, Colonel William Colmore, was prominent in the defence of Coventry.

During the reign of Henry VI, Sir Thomas Erdington and his wife Joyce had founded a chantry in Erdington in order for one priest to offer a daily service. This also suffered, and after the Dissolution the lands belonging to the chantry were given to a Richard Pallady and Francis Foxall, and later to Thomas Hawkins.

La Ford crossed the River Rea close to Kings Norton and was probably there before the Romans arrived, but they used it as a crossing for Ryknield Street. It eventually became known as Lifford and here could be found a monastery. This building was destroyed during the Dissolution and later, in 1604, Lifford Hall was built in its place. It is not recorded who built it but by 1781 it was the home of James Hewitt, the Chancellor of Ireland, who became Viscount Lifford.

A DASTARDLY DEED TO END A DYNASTY

Born in 1497, Edward Bermingham succeeded to the estates at the age of 3. His father had died so he inherited from his grandfather, Sir William de Bermingham. A wardship was granted by Henry VII, giving Lord Edward Dudley custody of the estates during Edward's minority. But when it came time for Edward to take charge of his inheritance the wardship was now in the hands of John Dudley, the 1st Duke of Northumberland. He was an ambitious man and wanted to keep the manor for himself. He offered to buy it, but Edward refused. Undeterred, Dudley made a plan that would make him the winner and Edward the loser.

While out riding one day, Edward met up with some other riders. They struck up a conversation with him and then rode alongside him. Unknown to Edward, another man was waiting further along the road for the group to arrive and they all had their instructions from Dudley. Meeting up with their accomplice, the men with Edward attacked and robbed him and rode off.

Reporting the robbery, the man told the authorities it was Edward who had attacked him. Of course, the other men were never found, so Edward alone stood trial. His lands were confiscated, and he was sentenced to be executed for the crime. Once Dudley had persuaded the king to pass the manor to him, he also pleaded for Edward's release. Edward was pardoned and given compensation of £40 per year. But that was the end of the Bermingham family's influence in Birmingham.

When Northumberland was executed following his involvement in the Lady Jane Grey plot, the manor became the property of the Crown. In 1555, it was acquired by Thomas Marrow of Berkeswell, but the manor house remained unoccupied and was left in a state of disrepair.

THE FOUNDING OF A SCHOOL

When Henry VIII died, his young son became King Edward VI, and it is thought that in compensation for his father's wrongdoings, Edward founded the Free Grammar School, which 300 years later became known as King Edward VI's Grammar School. At that time in 1552, Birmingham was still quite a small town, and nobody would have thought it would grow in the way that it did, so there was no doubt a degree of surprise that a prestigious school was being built there. Sited on land in New Street that was previously owned by the Guild of the Holy Cross, it was equipped to educate seventy boys – 100 years later it was educating 200 boys.

In the 1730s it was demolished and rebuilt to a larger size. Then, in the 1930s, with Birmingham having developed rapidly, being in the centre of Birmingham was no longer an option for the school, so 50 acres of land were found in Edgbaston and a new, larger school built there. This is where it still stands today but, of course, it is no longer just a boys' school.

A STREET FOR LOVE

In the late 1500s John Cooper donated a croft for use on 'love-days'. This was a day that had been set aside since medieval times to settle arguments and disputes between neighbours. The croft was about 4 acres in size and eventually made way for Loveday Street that, when you type the name into any UK map online, seems to be the only one in existence, despite love-days being held all over the country.

THE MARKET TOWN BEGINS TO GROW

In 1627, a visitor to Birmingham said the town was inhabited by blacksmiths, who forged all sorts of iron utensils and tools. Being so close to the villages in the area that was to become known as the Black Country, where the iron and coal industries had been developing since the 1400s, put Birmingham in a good position to become a manufacturer of metal goods. So, by the late sixteenth and early seventeenth centuries, the iron trade was beginning to flourish. In fact, the number of iron merchants in Birmingham equalled, in proportion, those in London.

As the seventeenth century progressed, the number of forges in the town increased. By 1683 there were 202; an increase of about 120 in ten years. But smaller metal trades also existed in Birmingham – buckles, scythes, knives, pewters, locks, nails and wire were all being made here.

A lot of families became very rich at this time. One family who became wealthy in the iron industry were the Jennens family. They became wealthy enough for John Jennens to buy the old Erdington Hall in 1650 and replace it with a new brick three-storey mansion with Dutch gables. John died in 1653 and his son, Humphrey, developed the Jennens' furnaces at Bromford, near the hall, and as well as living at the hall he also had a mansion along the High Street.

FAMILY FEUD

The Smallbrokes and the Colmores were old-established families, so a wedding between the two should have been the coming together of two dynasties. But was it?

Thomas Smallbroke had married Elizabeth Colmore in 1570 and ever since there had been arguments regarding the marriage settlement, and for many years there had been lawsuits to resolve the issue. The tension between the two families could be quite tense and by the early 1600s became violent. On one occasion, a woman told that while hanging out her washing, Thomas, his brother Richard and a servant ran past being chased by three members of the Colmore family. Firing their guns at the Smallbrokes, they missed, hitting the washing instead and causing a few holes in the garments on the line.

Scandalous leaflets were distributed about the Smallbrokes, and Thomas was attacked again. Another time, he was inspecting a barn on his farm in Bordesley when he was struck on the head by a member of the Colmore family.

Thomas Smallbroke now asked the town constable to arrest members of the Colmore family. He was hesitant, but Sir Thomas Holte intervened, and the case was submitted to the summer assizes. However, the Colmores bribed the witnesses, so Smallbroke had to take his complaint to the Court of the Star Chamber. The case cost him £700 and although the Colmores were fined, the money was never paid.

TYRANNY IN KING'S NORTON

From 1616 to 1623, the minister at King's Norton was Nathaniel Bradshaw. He strongly opposed drinking during the period when church services were taking place and reported innkeepers and customers alike to the Diocese of Worcester. The accused took reprisals, and Bradshaw was attacked and his house ransacked. Local landowner George Middlemore was one of the main assailants and he had also attacked schoolmaster Tobias Gyles.

Gyles spent quite a bit of time in London, neglecting his duties as a schoolmaster. On one October morning in 1625, a group, including Middlemore, broke into the school with the intention of evicting Gyles. However, he wasn't there.

The feud between Gyles and Middlemore continued for four years and ended with Gyles eventually losing his job, although he did remain as curate at the church. Perhaps as an act of defiance, he agreed to marry Middlemore's son, Robert, to Moseley heiress Eleanor Fox in a clandestine marriage in Hazelwell Hall one night. For this he did lose his curacy.

The Reverend Thomas Hall of King's Norton hated the long hair worn by the Royalists and was a devout Puritan. He was the preacher at the church and headmaster of the Old Grammar School from 1629 to 1662, and ran the school with a rod of iron. His students came from all parts of the country, and were intelligent young men, many of whom went on to university. But some of them would have fit easily into the student hooliganism we occasionally hear of today. The old tradition of 'barring out' involved the headmaster being shut out of his own school – usually by the door being barred – and not let in until he agreed some form of reward such as a half-day holiday. By the nineteenth century, this tradition was more controlled but in the seventeenth century it could end as a free-for-all and fights could easily ensue. On one occasion, Thomas Hall had his teeth knocked out in a scuffle.

A similar occurrence took place at the Birmingham Grammar School on 26 November 1667. Once again, pupils shut the headmaster outside, but later, when they themselves tried to gain entrance, they found the headmaster was inside and had shut them out. They threw stones and bricks and threatened to kill him. Local people even joined in. When the fun was over, the outcome was that a new school rule was added – if pupils practised barring out again they would be expelled.

THIRTEEN GABLES, UNLUCKY FOR SOME

In 1630, Pype Hayes Hall was built by Sir Hervey Bagot. The Bagot family had lived in Staffordshire since the eleventh century, but it was Hervey Bagot who became prominent in 1626 as High Sheriff of Staffordshire and was given a baronetcy in 1627.

The Birmingham connection starts with his second-born son, Hervey Bagot, who married Dorothy Arden. Conflicting reports say his father bought the land in Erdington, previously owned by Henry de Pype during the fourteenth century, for his son. Other reports say the land was part of the dowry of Dorothy Arden. However, Pype Hayes Hall became the home of the young married couple.

Hervey's brother, Richard, became a colonel in the Royalist army and as Governor of Lichfield had kept the Roundheads at bay, successfully defending that city and its celebrated cathedral. But he wasn't so lucky at Naseby. This well-known battle saw what became known as Parliament's New Model Army, led by Sir Thomas Fairfax and Oliver Cromwell, defeat the king's men. Richard was killed in action.

In the mid-1800s the house became known as the House of the Thirteen Gables. It was then occupied by the Reverend Egerton Arden Bagot, who made numerous changes to the house.

PLAGUE!

On 28 September 1631, the Justices of the Peace advised the Sheriff that plague had broken out in Deritend and was spreading towards Birmingham. It was thought that it had been brought there in a box of clothes on a coach from London. It is believed that to prevent the churchyards from being filled up, a piece of waste ground in Ladywood, about an acre in size, was used to bury the dead. The truth of this is debatable, because when houses were built in that area during the 1800s no bodies were found while digging the foundations.

A COSTLY VENTURE

In 1632, Sir Richard Grevis built Moseley Hall on land that had been acquired by his family, also known as Greaves, after the Dissolution. Sir Richard had been High Sheriff of Worcestershire and held manors in Yardley and Solihull. Previously, there had been a large half-timbered manor house at Moseley and remnants of this were found in the 1800s.

The building of the new hall proved costly for the Grevis family, and they suffered financial loss during the ensuing years. So much so that the last in the line, many years after the hall and land had been sold, was a simple labourer who lived on Edgbaston Street. He died in a gravel pit in Birmingham and was buried in a pauper's grave.

CIVIL WAR AND BIRMINGHAM

When Civil War broke out, Birmingham was sympathetic to Parliament and provided them with guns and swords. But when Charles I requested some, he was refused. However, there were a few families who supported the Royalist cause – the Holte family, for example. The king spent two nights at Aston Hall in October 1642 before moving on to Packwood. Later, his consort, Queen Henrietta, passed through the town on 10 July 1643 on her way to meet Prince Rupert at King's Norton. Travelling with her were 5,000 men she had recruited in Yorkshire. It is thought she stayed at the Saracen's Head and her men camped on land behind the church.

During that October in 1642, on the 18th, King Charles I inspected his Staffordshire troops on the edge of Sutton Park prior to the Battle of Edgehill. The spot later became known as Kingstanding.

Then, prior to the Battle of Naseby in 1645, the Royalist army camped somewhere in the vicinity of where Cannon Hill Park is today. In fact, it is said that that is how it got its name.

KING'S NORTON GETS INVOLVED

Following his visit to Aston Hall, King Charles travelled south. Somewhere around the King's Norton area, some of his carriages, which he wasn't travelling with, were attacked and the contents were taken to the Parliamentarian-controlled Warwick Castle.

Meanwhile, on 17 October, Prince Rupert, who had been resting in Stourbridge following the Battle of Powick, moved on to join the king with a troop of horses and 300 foot soldiers. Also on the road was Lord Willoughby, who was travelling to meet up with the Earl of Essex. The two sides inadvertently encountered each other, again around the King's Norton area. Obviously, they didn't just ride away, and the ensuing skirmish caused the deaths of over fifty Royalists and twenty Parliamentarians before Rupert and Willoughby continued on their way to their respective leaders.

BIRMINGHAM IN THE THICK OF IT

In 1643, Prince Rupert marched from Oxford with two objectives – to restore royal authority in Lichfield and to rebuke the Birmingham people for their disloyalty. He stayed at the Old Ship Inn, where it is thought he felt safe because underground tunnels in the cellars would help him escape if necessary. His troops camped nearby on a hill looking over the town. And this is how Camp Hill got its name.

On 3 April 1643, his troops of 1,200 horse and 700 foot attacked Birmingham in the early afternoon, entering from the Stratford and Alcester roads. The small Parliamentarian troop of 140 musketeers defending Birmingham, led by Captain Thomas Grevis of Moseley Hall, were assisted by numerous townsfolk who quickly built barricades across Bordesley High Street. The Cavaliers quickly broke down these defences but were fired on from the houses they passed. So, they set those houses on fire and the street fighting commenced, which continued in Deritend. The workers fought outside their workshops and homes before being put to the sword and their buildings set on fire. Several inhabitants were killed and nearly eighty houses were burned down.

Also involved was Basil Feilding, the Earl of Denbigh. He came up against a troop of Parliamentarian horse led by Captain Grevis and chased them towards Smethwick. But Feilding was killed, supposedly from a musket ball fired by Captain Grevis himself, so the Parliamentarians fled in all directions.

Prince Rupert now ordered his soldiers to burn and plunder the town. They rampaged along Bull Street and by nightfall, one tenth of the town was ablaze. What became known as the Battle of Birmingham caused £30,000 worth of damage. One victim was Robert Porter, of the Town Mill in Digbeth, who had supplied the Parliamentary army with 15,000 swords. His mill was destroyed.

Having had their revenge, the Royalists moved on to Lichfield. But the Birmingham parliamentarians eventually had their revenge too. Eight months later, the townspeople of Birmingham joined forces with a party of Roundheads and captured Aston Hall.

A Family House Taken by the Enemy

Richard Middlemore was a Royalist and he lost Edgbaston Hall during the Civil War. It was captured by Colonel John Fox, a tinker from Walsall. Fox marched into the hall with sixteen men and with the help of 200 metal workers from Birmingham, reinforced the hall's security using metal from the church roof. The lead from the church roof was also stripped and melted down to make bullets. Eventually given back to Robert Middlemore after the restoration, money was collected for the rebuilding of the church.

Then in 1688, when William of Orange became King of England, rioters from Birmingham burned down the hall to prevent it from becoming a sanctuary for Catholics.

After Robert's death, the estate was divided between his two granddaughters and sold to Sir Richard Gough, who rebuilt the manor house and church in 1717–18.

A FAMILY BUSINESS THRIVES

In 1650 John Onions set up his bellows-making business. It was one in which his descendants were still involved 200 years later when they amalgamated with William Allday & Co. in 1889. By then, they had become an engineering company and by the twentieth century they were making centrifugal fans. The name Onions was lost in 1969 when the company joined J.C. Peacock and became known as Alldays, Peacock & Co. Ltd.

A FAMILY FEUD

Thomas Holte was born in 1571 and was a member of the party that welcomed James I to England. He became a Sheriff of the County, was knighted by King James in 1603 and then in 1612 he bought, at a cost of £1,095, the baronetcy of Ulster and became a baronet. He now felt it was necessary to have a grand house and so built the majestic Aston Hall.

Work began in April 1618 but wasn't completed until April 1635, although he started to live there in 1631. When completed, it was described as the most stunning building in the area.

As he was too old to fight during the Civil War, he helped the cause financially and the king stayed for two nights at Aston Hall on 16 and 17 October 1642 before the Battle of Edge Hill. The following year, on 26 December 1643, Cromwell's men attacked the house but, protected by forty musketeers from Dudley Castle, Holte managed to hold off the 1,200 Parliamentarians for three days before having to surrender. Sixty of the enemy had been killed but he had lost twelve of his own men. He was taken prisoner and the hall was plundered. The eventual fines and confiscations cost him around £20,000.

Sir Thomas Holte died in 1654 and left a fund for the building of a hospital for five men and five women. Over the door of the almshouse, a plaque displayed the Holte coat of arms with the inscription:

> This Almshouse was (by the Charity of Sir Thomas Holte, late of this town, and County Knight and Baronet Deceased) provided for and appointed to be built and was in order thereto accordingly erected by his grandson and heir Sir Robert Holte in the year of our Lord 1655 and 1656. Laus Deo.

The almshouse was demolished in 1930.

Thomas' son Edward was a Groom of the Bedchamber of King Charles I and joined him during the Civil War. He fought in the Battle of Edge Hill, where he was wounded. In August 1643, he was in Oxford when it was besieged. He became ill with a fever and had died before the town surrendered, so when Sir Thomas died, it was Edward's son, Robert, who succeeded.

However, Thomas had not wanted his son, Edward, to inherit the estate. This was because Edward had wanted to marry the daughter of Dr John King, Bishop of London, and Sir Thomas wouldn't give his permission. Edward ignored his father and married her anyway. Sir Thomas was furious his son had disobeyed him and threatened to disinherit him, but Charles I intervened. He wrote to Sir Thomas telling of his great respect for Edward and that he considered his son had married the daughter of a good and much-revered man. He ended by saying that Sir Thomas should 'forbeare any act against your sonne in respect of his match' and 'restore him into your former favour and good opinion'. Thomas may have restored Edward's inheritance but the rift between father and son remained and the only time Edward visited the family home again was as a member of Charles I's entourage during his visit to Aston Hall.

Edward wasn't the only child of Sir Thomas to suffer. When their mother, Grace Bradbourne, had died, Sir Thomas had married Anne Littleton of Pillaton. It is said that Anne disliked one of her stepdaughters and persuaded Thomas to lock her up until she went mad.

Another daughter – or perhaps it is the same daughter – tells her story in letters that are still on show at the hall. Elizabeth Mary fell in love with one of the servants, Francis, and it seems they planned to run away together. But Sir Thomas discovered their secret and began making arrangements for a suitable marriage for Elizabeth. Shortly afterwards, Francis disappeared. Some say he was murdered, others that he committed suicide by hanging himself in the Great Parlour, and his body was disposed of in some way. Elizabeth also died before a marriage could be arranged. It is said that while trying to escape after being locked in her room, she fell down the stairs.

Hope of Atonement

The Holte Almshouse previously mentioned was said to have been built as a kind of atonement for the murder of Sir Thomas' cook. Described as an arrogant, selfish and cruel man, Sir Thomas was also well known for boasting about how punctual his cook was. One day, he had a wager with friends he had gone hunting with that their dinner would be ready when they returned. But unfortunately, for whatever reason, his cook did not live up to expectations and the meal wasn't ready. Sir Thomas not only lost his wager but had to suffer the mockery given to him by his companions. Seized with rage he went into the kitchen, grabbed a cleaver and hit the cook across the head with it.

The truth of this is shown in a court hearing in 1606, when Sir Thomas had taken out a writ against William Ascrick for broadcasting this story. Ascrick gave quite a description of the incident, adding that the cook's head was split in half and the two sides fell onto each shoulder. Sir Thomas asked for £1,000 in damages but only received £30 1*s* for his costs.

So, did the incident happen? By the fact that Sir Thomas received a royal pardon from King Charles I for crimes and accusation of crimes committed prior to 27 March 1625 (the day King James died), it certainly seems he could have been capable of anything.

Rebuilding Lives

After the restoration, Robert Holte was rewarded for the family's loyalty and made High Sheriff of Warwickshire and a Knight of the Shire. As High Sheriff, his duties would be to inspect the market and rectify weights and dry measures, make proclamations announcing the two fairs each year and hold dinners for other officers and dignitaries.

During the war the family had suffered financially, even to the extent that Robert had spent time in the Fleet Debtors' Prison. However, his only son and successor, Charles, had married Jane, the daughter of Lord Brereton of Brereton Hall in Cheshire, and with her came a large inheritance from that side of the family that replenished the family fortunes.

FIRES IN RELIGIOUS HOUSES

Once the Declaration of Independence was passed in 1672, the Nonconformists in Birmingham quickly took advantage of now being able to worship openly in their own religious buildings – apart from Catholics, who were only allowed to meet for Mass in their own homes and houses. Within no time, two Nonconformist chapels had been erected: the Old Meeting House, as it became known, in Dudley Street and another in Digbeth.

However, in 1687 the Catholic church of St Mary Magdalen and St Francis was erected. The foundation stone was laid on 23 March. The following year, on 16 August, the first stone was laid to build a Franciscan convent next to the church.

But the life of the church was short. It was burned down on 26 November 1688 on the orders of Lord Dellamer during the Exclusion Crisis – a period when bills were brought to Parliament that tried to save England from the possibility of King Charles II's brother, James, inheriting the throne because he was Catholic. The priests found shelter in Harborne at the Catholic church in Pritchett's Lane and for the next 100 years, the small number of Catholic congregation worshipped here.

In 1715, the Old Meeting House was burned down by Church of England protesters, who would have also attacked the Digbeth Chapel had they not been dissuaded by the offer of drink from the minister. A new meeting house was built in Moor Street in 1732.

A NEW ORDER FOR GUNS

Guns were being made in Birmingham in the early 1600s, but it wasn't a thriving industry at first. It was King William III who gave the gun industry in Birmingham a kick-start.

One day, he was overheard complaining that the only decent guns he could find were in Holland and they were costly. It was the Member of Parliament for Warwickshire, Sir Richard Newdigate, who overheard the conversation. Obtaining a gun from a gunmaker in Digbeth, he took it to show the king. The king liked the look of it and placed a large order. When everyone found out how happy the king was with his guns, they all wanted guns from Birmingham. And so the industry flourished.

Centred around Digbeth, this area became known as the Gun Quarter and many gunmakers soon became wealthy. However, gunmaking did make difficulties for one shop owner. Samuel Galton was a member of the Society of Friends. They abhorred violence and told him he must give up his business. He refused and was therefore disowned by them.

BIRMINGHAM IN THE 1700S

By the late 1600s, the population of Birmingham was growing rapidly, and the steel goods now being made – such as swords, heads of canes and snuffboxes – were said to be of the highest quality. The industrialists involved in these trades were becoming wealthy middle-class people.

As the century progressed, the town was also to benefit from better transport and the rapidly developing Black Country and its iron-making, but for now, Birmingham was still just a country town with its manor house surrounded by a moat. Paradise Street was just a road through fields. Easy Hill,

With its rows of cruck houses similar to these, Birmingham still looked like a country town.

Summer Hill, Newhall Hill, Ludgate Hill, Constitution Hill and Snow Hill were all just fields – and New Street was just a new street with a few cottages.

By the late 1750s, Birmingham had not only become a great middle-class town, it had also become a place of freedom. There were numerous opportunities in a variety of trades and industries, and it was also a place of freedom for many creeds and cultures other than the Established Church. Many types of Dissenters flocked to the town – Baptists, Catholics, Jews and Quakers all found homes there.

THE DEVELOPMENT OF A NEW TOWN

Birmingham consisted of fifteen streets in 1650, with 900 houses and 5,472 inhabitants. This figure had risen from the previous 100 years, when the population had been 3,500. But the 1700s saw further expansion. In 1700, there were twenty-eight streets, with 100 courts and alleys and 15,032 inhabitants. Thirty years later, there were fifty-five streets, 150 courts and alleys with 23,286 inhabitants.

Development began around the Old Square in 1697, which consisted of several two-storey brick houses. In 1709, Temple Street was built, followed in 1715 by Temple Row. Cherry Street and Cannon Street both appeared in 1733 and in 1747 work began on the Newhall estate around Colmore Row. Henry Bradford advertised that he would give a freehold site to anyone who would build a house there. That subsequent street became known as Bradford Street.

More houses began to appear along New Street, which in those times extended to Suffolk Street. The lease on the land here included a covenant stating that after 100 years the lease would expire, and the ground was to be handed back to the Grammar School complete with all its crops of potatoes. But when that lease did expire, the area had been built up to such an extent that the clause was impossible to adhere to.

Over seventy years, the population and the number of houses grew rapidly, as the following shows:

	Houses	Population
1741	4,114	24,660
1773	7,369	30,804
1778	8,042	48,252
1781	8,382	50,295
1801	16,659	78,760
1811	19,096	85,755

It was at the end of the eighteenth century that surveyor John Snape drew up a plan of the town. Using the same scale of other maps in England, it was then discovered that Birmingham was the largest town in England.

A NEW CHURCH FOR THE GROWING POPULATION

With the growth of Birmingham, it became evident that the parish church of St Martin's couldn't accommodate all those who still worshipped in the Established Church. So, a decision was made to build a second church in another part of the expanding town. Four acres of land at Horse Close, known as 'Mr Phillips barley close', was given by Elizabeth Phillips and her son and daughter-in-law, Mr and Mrs William Phillips Inge, for the building of the new church.

St Philip's was designed by Thomas Archer of Umberslade Hall, Hockley Heath, and although it was not completed until 1719, it was consecrated in 1715. It was built of sandstone from Rowington but had to be refaced with harder sandstone from Staffordshire in the 1860s. Now Birmingham's cathedral, it still has the ambiance of a parish church.

To help finance the building, the commissioners gave £5,000 and Sir Richard Gough managed to persuade George I to give £600 towards the completion of the tower. A weathervane was erected showing the Gough family's crest as a thank you.

Further churches were built during the 1700s. In 1735, a new church was built in Deritend as a chapel of ease for Aston. It replaced St John's Chapel, which had been founded in 1378. Following this in 1749, John Jennens gave St Bartholomew's, which was built in the centre of a large burial ground, as a gift.

In 1774, Mrs Weaman gifted St Mary's Chapel and in 1779, Charles Colmore gave land for the building of St Paul's Chapel. A spire was added in 1823.

With the ever-increasing population over the next century, other churches were built, one of which was St Barnabas Church on Ryland Street. Built in 1859–60, it was decorated in a Gothic style to designs by architect William Bourne, at a cost of £3,000.

THE HOLDEN FAMILY

The Holden family had lived at the Old Hall in Wood End, in the manor of Erdington, now known as Pype Hayes, for many years, and for many generations were rangers for Sutton Chase. First given the post by Edward IV, it was abolished by Henry VIII, but the family remained in Erdington.

When Humphrey Holden died in 1705, he was survived by three sons. At first, his eldest son, Henry, inherited the estate. He was a doctor and Senior Fellow of Magdalen College in Oxford, but he died five years later without issue.

His brother James was living in Faro, Portugal, and had been a consul in the 'Kingdom of Algarve' for the last seventeen years. It was said he had shown himself to be very loyal to both queen and country and very charitable in supplying financial assistance to English prisoners to help them return home. But now he had to return home himself to take up his inheritance. Unfortunately, he caught a cold on the journey home, developed dropsy, and died on 27 February 1712, again with no issue.

The estate now passed to Humphrey's third son, Robert. He married and provided an heir to take over when he died in 1730.

MORE TROUBLE IN THE HOLTE FAMILY

Sir Cloberry Holte, the 4th Baronet of Aston, married Barbara Lister in 1719, but it doesn't seem to have been a happy marriage as he described her as never being home, and when she was, she was never satisfied. His mother didn't like her either and thought she was a bad influence. After Cloberry died in 1729 aged 48, Barbara was only allowed to visit her children and Aston Hall for two weeks a year.

Clobery wrote in his will that his 'honoured mother, Ann Holte' was to be 'guardian of my children'. If his mother died before the children reached their majority, they were to be placed in the care of his brother.

ANOTHER FAMILY DYNASTY

In 1717, Sir Richard Gough, an eminent East India Merchant and Member of Parliament, bought the manor of Edgbaston from Lady Bridget Fauconberg and rebuilt the hall. At the time, Edgbaston just consisted of a few scattered farms and houses, but Sir Richard's descendants would eventually change all that.

His son, Henry was also a merchant with the East India Company, and in 1725 he was accepted into the Inner Temple. He first married Catherine Harpur, the daughter of Sir John Harpur of Calke in Derbyshire, but she died in 1740, so he then married Barbara Calthorpe, an heiress from Hampshire. Her family also had estates in Norfolk.

Their son, also Henry, inherited the estates when his father died in 1774, but when his maternal uncle died in 1788, he also received an inheritance from his mother's family. Therefore, he took both names, becoming Henry Gough-Calthorpe. In 1796, he was created Baron Calthorpe. His son, George, who became the 3rd Lord Calthorpe following the death of his brother Charles, carried the Gold Spurs at the coronation of George IV on 19 July 1821.

In the early 1800s the Gough-Calthorpe family could see the benefit of turning their lands into new developments. Building on the Calthorpe Estate began around 1810 and the largest part was built between the 1830s and 1870s. However, there were stipulations. Only wanting to attract wealthy merchants and industrialists, Lord Calthorpe refused the building of small houses. With a price range that only the middle to high classes could afford, the tree-lined roads contained attractive houses with tennis courts, croquet lawns, rose gardens and shrubberies. There were to be no substandard buildings and definitely no factories to spoil the view or anywhere within the scent of their wealthy residents.

Eventually, the hall built by Sir Richard Gough became the clubhouse for Edgbaston Golf Club.

PATENTS

On 22 May 1722, Richard Baddeley, an ironmonger, was the first Birmingham inventor to receive a patent. His invention was a new method for casting wheel streaks that were more durable than those made of iron. But he also invented the box iron – a new home utensil that would make it easier for the women of the house to smooth out the wrinkles of the family's clothes. The base of the iron block was hollow where hot coals could be placed to heat the bottom so it would glide across the clothes, ironing out the creases.

Following Richard Baddeley, ninety-two other inventors were granted patents by the end of the century. However, the following century saw many more patents being taken out:

1810s	71
1820s	83
1830s	170
1840s	265

THE BLUE COAT SCHOOL

The Blue Coat School (so named for the distinctive uniform worn by pupils) was opened in 1724 by the Reverend William Higgs, the first Rector of St Philip's, close to the church. It educated and clothed twenty-two boys and ten girls when it first opened, but 150 years later, these figures had risen to 150 boys and 100 girls. They were taught writing, arithmetic, reading, sewing and knitting and had separate playgrounds at the side of the school.

Money for the school was raised by special services being preached in churches, chapels and other places of worship every six months, followed by a collection. People also left legacies in their wills. The first person to do this was Mrs Elizabeth White, who left the school nearly 30 acres of land. Worth about £250 per annum, the land was used as investment for the school.

Past pupils also contributed to the upkeep of the school having formed a society called Truth Blues.

BELL RINGERS

William Blews was a brass worker and started Blews & Son at Holloway Head in 1732. It remained in business until around 1900. As makers of candlesticks, bells and weights, they exhibited at the Great Exhibition in 1851. Many of their church bells are still being rung across the country today.

THE UNLUCKY INVENTOR

Although Lancashire is famous for cotton spinning and mills, cotton was being spun in a small house near Sutton Coldfield in the early 1700s. John Wyatt was born in Weeford, near Lichfield, in 1700. He was a carpenter by trade but dabbled with various inventions. One such invention was a machine for cutting files, which Birmingham gunsmith Richard Heeley provided finance for. But the money ran out before the machine was perfected. Lewis Paul of London took the project up, but again, it was dropped a year later.

Wyatt had a shed in Sutton Coldfield where he built his spinning machine. Then, in 1744, he set it up in his warehouse in Birmingham at Upper Priory. However, the patent had been taken out by his old partner and financier, Lewis Paul, so he gained nothing from the invention, which was later improved by Richard Arkwright, who then received all the recognition.

His other inventions included lightning conductors, lathes and fire-extinguishing machines. Eventually ending up in debtors' prison, he used his time there to work on drawings for a compound-lever weighbridge. This proved successful and one was installed outside the workhouse in Snow Hill. As their popularity grew, they also became larger. The first one was 10ft in length with a capacity of 6 tons, but when Avery's began making them at their Soho factory, the largest one was 60ft in length with a capacity of 400 tons.

A YOUNG MAN WITH A FUTURE

In 1741, an 18-year-old youth arrived in Birmingham from Nottingham. He had worked as a weaver's apprentice but had absconded from work to go to Nottingham Races. His employer, who was also his uncle, was not at all happy, so to escape his uncle's tyranny the young man ran away.

He arrived at Hamstead Heath just as the sun was setting over Birmingham and was spellbound by the view – in particular, the glowing building that was St Philip's Church.

Making his way into town, he sat down by the Old Cross where two men bought him some bread and cheese and a jug of ale at the Bell Inn in Philip Street. They then found him somewhere to stay the night.

That young man was William Hutton, who became Birmingham's celebrated and well-thought-of historian. However, he left when he was unable to find work on this first visit.

Nine years later, he returned and set up a bookshop as well as taking up book binding and publishing. He quickly became a success and married Sarah Cook on 23 July 1755 in the church he had fallen in love with on his first visit. In 1769, he bought half an acre of land at Bennett's Hill and built Red Hill House. He also had a go at farming, buying a farm at Stetchford, which he regularly visited.

Then in 1780, he began writing the book that was going to make him famous, and the now well-known *History of Birmingham* was published on 22 March 1782. Four updated editions were published in total, plus an edition was published after his death by James Guest. The book is still read today.

Following the publication of the book, Hutton became an authority on the history of Birmingham, but he also became a victim of the Priestley Riots when the mob attacked his shop, throwing his papers and prints into the muddy street outside.

When William Hutton died in 1815, his daughter, Catherine, completed the book he was writing about his life. Following in her father's footsteps, she had become a writer and penned several novels.

Ironically, Hutton was, at one time, one of the commissioners for the Court of Requests. This was held in a room over the Old Cross where, many years earlier, he had sat with no money and no prospects.

ANOTHER CASE OF MIXED LOYALTIES

In July 1745, Charles Edward Stuart landed on the coast of Scotland with the intention of fighting his way through the country to regain the crown of England as the grandson of James II. The whole country prepared itself, and without doubt, Birmingham did the same. He never got as far as Birmingham, but Sir Lister Holte had formed a regiment of 250 volunteers to pursue the rebels, should they reach the town. Ironically, the great-grandfather of the young pretender Charles I had been a guest of an ancestor of Sir Lister.

The prince did have one friend in Birmingham though – Charles Jennens, the grandson of Humphrey Jennens who, although a Protestant, did support the deposed Catholic monarchy. Swords were even made in Birmingham for Bonnie Prince Charlie, should he need them on his arrival. So, despite Sir Lister Holte's volunteers, there were others who would have welcomed him.

FAMILIES INVEST IN NEW STREETS

Mary Sherlock was the sister of Thomas Sherlock, who, at one time, had been the Bishop of London. He had bought various estates from the Marrow family, who had acquired the Birmingham manor after the demise of the de Bermingham family.

Mary had married Thomas Gooch, whose family had originated from Suffolk, and as Thomas Sherlock's heir, she inherited the lands he owned in Birmingham. With the growth of Birmingham so evident, Thomas Gooch quickly saw the advantage of developing on these lands and eventually streets with such names as Gooch Street, Sherlock Street, Bishop Street and Suffolk Street were born.

Another family who gave their name to the developing town of Birmingham were the Colmores. In 1747, Ann Colmore, the widow of Charles Colmore, divided the Colmore estate into building plots and Ann Street, Colmore Row, Edmund Street, Great Charles Street and Little Charles Street were created. Edmund Street was named after her brother-in-law, Great Charles Street after her son and Little Charles Street after her husband. She then handed over the estate to her son, Charles, and retired to Bath.

Charles gave land for the building of St Paul's Churchyard and, later, for the building of St Thomas' Church in Bath Row. His children were also immortalised in the names of Birmingham streets – Lionel, Mary Ann and Caroline.

Charles died in 1794, and the estate passed to his three children, none of whom married, and by 1825 Caroline was the sole survivor of the estate. Her father had added a codicil to his will saying that if his children died without issue, the estate should pass to the Hertford family of Ragley Hall, Francis Hertford being his 'dear friend'. So, Caroline applied to the Court of Chancery to release part of the estate. In 1829, the estate was divided between her and the 3rd Marquess of Hertford, Francis' grandson. And when she died in 1837, aged 70, her share of the estate went to her friend, Frind Cregoe.

AS BOLD AS BRASS

There was a brass industry in Birmingham as early as 1668 and a brass foundry was established by Walter Tippin and Henry Carver in 1715. But it was in the mid-1700s that the industry really took off, following a brass works being opened in Coleshill Street by John and William Turner. Within a few decades Birmingham was the main supplier of brass.

At first, only small items were made, such as pots and dishes, but the industry grew and grew and soon anything that could be made from brass was. There were small items, like pipe fittings, or large items such as bedsteads. Anything from useful to ornamental items were made and workers began to flock from all over the country to work in Birmingham's brass industry.

THE FOLLY OF EDGSBASTON

Standing 96ft high, with an attached spiral staircase, this six-storey tower was built by John Perrott in the gardens of his house at Icknield Street West, Edgbaston, in 1758. Originally from Belbroughton, Worcestershire, he had previously lived on the corner of Bull Street and Steelhouse Lane, but moved to Edgbaston so he could look across the fields and watch the hunt and hare coursing. Building this tall tower supposedly gave him a better view.

However, another story suggests he built the tower so he could spy on his unfaithful wife, who he was convinced was having an affair with the local gamekeeper. First known as the Monument, it soon became known as Perrott's Folly, and other theories say he used it to follow the sun during the day and the moon and stars at night as well as to entertain friends.

When glassmaker Abraham Osler lived in the house in the 1880s, he used the tower as an observation post for weather forecasting. From then on until 1979, it was known as the Edgbaston Observatory and was one of the world's first regular weather-forecasting establishments. Since then, it has been used by both the Birmingham & Midland Institute and the University of Birmingham.

John Perrott died in 1776, and his estate passed to his only child, Catherine, who had married Walter Noel in May 1765. Hence, two streets close to the tower took the names Noel Street and Monument Road.

Perrott's house has long since been demolished, but his tower still stands high above the houses around it.

WORTH THE WALK

In 1760, Aaron Atkin, a saw-maker, walked from Sheffield to Birmingham with his three sons, all carrying the tools of their trade with them. Alfred was also a saw-maker, Edwin was a toolmaker and George was a plane-maker. On arriving in Birmingham, they acquired a workshop in Ludgate Hill and set up a business as saw-makers. After moving locations a few times, the family business eventually ended up in Bradford Street, where it remained in the family until 1949.

Another business set up in 1760 whose founder had originally come from Sheffield was the refinery John Betts & Sons Ltd. Situated on the corner of Charlotte Street with St Paul's Square, it was founded by Alexander Betts. He and his son John arrived in Birmingham just as the jewellery trade was growing and literally grew their business from dust. In other words, the shavings swept up off the floors of the jewellery workshops. Their refinery then sorted out the dust from the particles of precious metals, gold and silver. After becoming a success in Birmingham, John sat as alderman on Birmingham's first town council.

BUTTONS, IRON AND BANKS

John Taylor was born in 1711 and worked as a cabinetmaker before becoming a manufacturer of buttons, buckles and snuffboxes. From his factory in Union Street, he specialised in gilt items, but also became a celebrated manufacturer of japanned articles. Japanning was a unique process of painting a surface with lacquer, which could be used on any surface – metal, leather, wood or papier-mâché. It could be of any colour, although black was the most popular, with tortoiseshell the next favourite.

Taylor became very successful, at one time employing 500 workers. He invested in property and in 1768 bought Moseley Hall from the Grevis family.

The Lloyd family had moved to Birmingham in 1664 from South Wales to avoid persecution as Quakers. Sampson Lloyd became an iron merchant, setting up shop in Edgbaston Street and his son, also Sampson, went on to build a slitting mill on the River Rea in Digbeth. The family home was a large house on Edgbaston Street, but they also owned property in Stourbridge and Leominster.

Together, John Taylor and Sampson Lloyd were to become famous in a different world to their respective businesses. In June 1765, they and their sons joined together to form Taylors & Lloyds Bank in Dale End, which was later to become known as Lloyds Bank.

BIRMINGHAM AND THE INDUSTRIAL REVOLUTION

On 26 March 1777, the House of Commons were debating a Bill to give the theatre in Birmingham a licence. Mr Burke, who was in favour of this, referred to Birmingham as 'the great toyshop of Europe'. Of course, he wasn't talking of the items children play with, but the small items that were manufactured in their thousands in Birmingham. Things such as snuffboxes, tinderboxes, candlesticks, buttons and buckles, pokers, fire shovels and tongs, hammers, pliers and corkscrews were all items that were considered either light steel toys or heavy steel toys.

THE MAN RESPONSIBLE?

It has always been said that the start of Birmingham's industrial revolution was all down to one man. Whether or not that is an unfavourable quote in respect of other industrialists, Matthew Boulton was certainly a genius who had a vision of how industry should advance.

In 1756, Edward Ruston leased from the lord of the manor a piece of land that lay between Nineveh and Hockley. He dug out Hockley Brook to make it deeper and built a small mill there. In 1764, Matthew Boulton bought this piece of ground from him and purchased the freehold.

Matthew's father, also named Matthew, was a hardware manufacturer and had left his son a considerable inheritance. So, at a cost of £10,000, although some records state it cost

The Soho Works.

£20,000, this barren heath, which previously had just been the home of numerous rabbits and a few beggars looking for a place to rest their heads at night, became the Soho Works.

Ten years later, this Georgian industrial estate was well established, with four square buildings and now the home of 1,000 workers in various workshops. And nearby was Soho House. Wanting to be close to his works, Boulton built himself a majestic house and here he entertained many dignified people, from lords and ladies to philosophers and scientists.

Boulton had started out as a 'toymaker' and became so successful that his premises in Snow Hill became too small, and seeing that other 'toymakers' and manufacturers were also becoming successful, his idea of having a dedicated place for industry was born. Many workers who were at the top of their trade were attracted by Boulton's idea and so the Soho Works developed an excellent reputation. The goods produced here were sold not only across the whole of Britain, but Europe too and eventually the world. And, although mass produced, they were all of high quality and new patterns and designs were being introduced regularly.

In 1769, Matthew Boulton met James Watt and steam was introduced to Soho. An iron foundry was also built out towards Smethwick, at the side of the Birmingham Canal, where they produced engines made from 1–200 horsepower.

Later, a mint was introduced to Soho, and with the help of steam engines, copper was rolled into sheets thin enough to use for coins. A contract with the East India Company was agreed; when this proved successful, Boulton approached other companies and soon he not only had contracts with them but with the British Government too. The Soho Mint remained in operation throughout the early 1800s and was handed down to his son and then his grandson. It finally closed in 1850 to make way for building developments.

In 1800, Matthew Boulton Jnr and James Watt Jnr took over the partnership from their fathers and Matthew Boulton died nine years later. He was buried at St Mary's, Handsworth, and the funeral procession included numerous friends and 600 workmen.

Boulton's Contemporaries

Socially, Matthew Boulton surrounded himself with a large crowd of like-minded people, which of course included James Watt.

Watt had been born in Scotland and became interested in the use of steam engines when working at Glasgow University as an instrument-maker and repairer. While repairing Newcomen's engine, he felt he could improve on it – which he did. And it was while he was promoting this new engine that he met Matthew Boulton. His home became Heathfield House, which he had built in Handsworth using the same architect, Samuel Wyatt, who had designed Soho House. He died on 25 August 1819 and is also buried at St Mary's in Handsworth.

Another contemporary was William Murdoch, who later changed his name to Murdock. He arrived at Soho looking for employment after walking 300 miles from the north. He was given a job in the pattern workshop. Proving himself an excellent worker, he progressed through the ranks and was sent to Cornwall to work on the building, maintenance and repair of Boulton and Watt's engines in the tin mines.

It was while he was living in Cornwall that he experimented with gas lighting. As a child, he had played with his mother's kettle, putting coal dust in it and setting fire to the steam coming out. Using this childhood game as a guide, he constructed a lighting system in his house. When Boulton and Watt heard about it, they asked him to develop his idea. At first, just two gas lamps were fitted at the Soho Works, but it wasn't long before the whole factory was lit. Murdoch went on to great things, eventually becoming a partner at the Soho Works.

Although the scientist Dr Joseph Priestley only lived in Birmingham for a short period of his life, he has always been adopted as a Brummie. A chemist, clergyman and political theorist, in 1773 he received the Copley Medal for discovering oxygen and nine other gases. He arrived in Birmingham in 1780 and became a preacher at the New Meeting House. He lived at Fair Hill, in Smallbrook, and set up a laboratory in the house. Eleven years later, he saw the Birmingham riots, often known as the Priestley Riots due to the fact they were aimed at Priestley and his congregation (see p74). His house and church were destroyed, so he left Birmingham and eventually emigrated to America in 1794.

The Galton family made their money in the gun-making business and then turned to banking. Samuel Galton was born in Bristol in 1719 and married into Birmingham's gun-making trade. His works were in Weaman Street and the mill, used for grinding and polishing the barrels and blades, was in Duddeston. He had a town house in Steelhouse Lane, but the family also owned Duddeston Hall. When in residence at the hall, Samuel Galton was known for going down to the lake, blowing a whistle, then feeding the assortment of ducks, geese and other water birds that would flock to him.

Samuel Jnr lived at Great Barr Hall and was excluded from the Society of Friends because he made guns. He married Lucy Barclay of the banking family, who at one time was notoriously known as the daughter of George III and the Quaker Hannah Lightfoot, although this has since been disproved.

Boulton's Eccentric Friend

In 1723, aged 17, John Baskerville arrived in Birmingham and found work as the servant for a clergyman, who recognised his writing skills. Becoming a teacher for the poor boys of the parish, he later taught writing and bookkeeping at King Edward's School. His interest in calligraphy and engraving stone found him pursuing this work in Edgbaston Church. Then japanning was introduced in Birmingham – and this gave Baskerville an idea.

Closely following John Taylor, who we mentioned in the previous chapter, Baskerville watched him purchase the materials he used for the varnishing of his goods. This way, he learned the ingredients and quantities, and by 1749 he was also well established in japanning. Through his ingenuity, he discovered many ways to improve the craft and his candlesticks, cake stands, salvers and other items made him very rich.

He built his house, Easy Hill, on an 8-acre site a quarter of a mile north-east of Birmingham and became very conspicuous by his flamboyant style. He travelled in a carriage of rich gilt with distinctive pictures, every panel being differently painted with little naked cupids and flowers. It was pulled by a pair of beautiful cream-coloured horses with net hangings almost touching the ground. He wore elaborate outfits. His favourite was said to be one of green with gold lace, worn with a scarlet waistcoat edged in broad, gold lace and a small, round hat edged with lace. He once attended a funeral in a bright-coloured suit trimmed with gold lace.

At the age of 50, having amassed a large fortune, he became interested in printing and spent £700 on apparatus and type, which he set up in his house. He constructed his own presses, spent time inventing his own fonts and his own recipe for ink. His first book, *Virgil*, was printed in 1757. Over the following sixteen years he printed sixty-seven books, including the family Bible of Matthew Boulton, to whom Baskerville had been a mentor.

In the 1750s, Sarah Eaves and her two daughters went to live with him at Easy Hill after her husband had left her without any money. Soon they were living as man and wife. She even called herself Mrs Baskerville. Once it was discovered that Mr Eaves had died, they married on 1 June 1764 at St Martin's Church.

True to his life, his death in 1775 was also unique. Having no time for religion, he didn't want to be buried in consecrated ground, so he was buried in his own garden. His will also instructed his executors to bury his books in the vault in a conical building he had erected in his grounds.

In 1789, Easy Hill was sold to John Ryland and during alterations Baskerville's coffin was moved to a warehouse where curious spectators visited regularly. Then, when Easy Hill was being used as a canal wharf, he was moved again. It was now thought he should be buried at St Philip's, but the rector refused on the grounds that Baskerville had been an atheist. Bookseller Mr Knott came to the rescue. He had a vault in Christ Church and said it would be an honour to have the remains buried there. When that church was demolished, John Baskerville was moved to Warstone Cemetery. The Baskerville font remains in widespread use to this day.

By the Light of the Moon

The Lunar Society met on the Monday nearest to a full moon so that members could travel home with a certain degree of light. Meetings were held at either Matthew Boulton's Soho House or Great Barr Hall, the home of Samuel Galton.

Soho House, the home of Matthew Boulton.

Started in 1765, it was a society where scientists, engineers and industrialists could meet over dinner to discuss new inventions, modern ideas and scientific experiments. With members including John Baskerville, Matthew Boulton, James Watt, Joseph Priestley, William Murdoch and Samuel Galton, it was an exclusive club with no more than fourteen members and very particular as to who could join, although visitors were allowed to join the meetings on the odd occasion to give their points of view. Such visitors included Thomas Jefferson, Richard Arkwright and Benjamin Franklin.

Near to Great Barr Hall, on the junction of Aldridge Road and Queslett Road, can be found 'the Moonstones'. Erected in 1998, these stone memorials depict members of the society and also show the different phases of the moon.

METHODISTS

John Wesley made his first visit to Birmingham in 1738, but on 21 March 1764 he opened the Moor Street Theatre as a place of worship for the Methodists. At one point they also used the King

Street Theatre, but this didn't prove popular with theatregoers. On one occasion, as the congregation were leaving after a service held by Wesley, they had stones thrown at them.

At a cost of £1,200, a new meeting house was built in Cherry Street and opened on 7 July 1782 by John Wesley. However, the new benches weren't strong enough to hold the large congregation and in the middle of Wesley's sermon a loud noise was heard. People had been standing on a bench to get a better view and it had broken. Luckily, no one was hurt.

Despite his age, Wesley visited Birmingham on a few more occasions, very often preaching to a crowd of 500. His last visit was in 1790.

A member of the Methodist family, Francis Asbury, was born in Hamstead in 1745 and his boyhood home was Asbury Cottage, Newton Road, Great Barr. After emigrating to America, he spent forty-five years working as a Methodist bishop.

STREETS AND ROADS

On 21 April 1769, following an Act for the improvement of town streets, the Street Commissioners were appointed. They were what was considered the first officials of local government, although they didn't have the type of power government officials have today. Their duties were mainly to care for the streets, organise repairs and cleanliness, and make sure the streets were lit and enough watchmen were employed to keep the peace.

In 1801, their work was extended to making major improvements, so they now organised for the streets around the Bull Ring to be widened. This work saw the demolition of nine tenements and then in 1806, the remaining houses and shops around St Martin's. They also organised the building of both the Town Hall and the Market Hall.

By 1828 there were eighty-nine Street Commissioners in Birmingham and their work for the remaining years of their power saw them building new roads, paving old streets and organising the markets. The Charter of Incorporation in 1838 took away their power but they continued to represent the town as a tradition until 31 December 1851.

While improvements were being made to the town's streets, the highways around the town could be dangerous places. Highwaymen lurked on the Chester, Coventry and Warwick roads, among others, and one area that was popular with highwaymen was Sutton Chase – it is even thought that Dick Turpin sometimes hung around here. Another highwayman, by the name of 'King', was born somewhere between Sutton and Stonnall, and the rumour has it that he was eventually caught and burned to death in Sutton Park. Gangs from Birmingham would also leave the town in the dead of night and terrorise the occupants of outlying farms and houses.

New Oscott was once known as Gibbett Hill and here the bodies of executed criminals would be hung high up for all to see as a warning not to pursue a life of crime.

A New Form of Transport

The winter of 1766–67 was very bad and heavy snow made it almost impossible for coaches and wagons to get into Birmingham. So, in January 1767, a group of businessmen met at The Swan to discuss alternative forms of transport. The Swan, on the High Street, was the main coaching inn in the 1700s. It disappeared when the area was redeveloped, although its name remained in Swan Passage. But this, too, was to disappear underneath the Bull Ring.

The roads into Birmingham were known as 'holloways', due to their bad condition. They contained deep ruts made by the constant use of wagons, stagecoaches and other horse-drawn vehicles. By July 1767, an Act of Parliament had paved the way for a canal to be cut between Birmingham and the coalfields of Staffordshire as an alternative. James Brindley was employed to make the survey and two years later, the 22-mile canal, costing £70,000, had been cut. The first load of coal arrived on 6 November 1769.

Other canals soon followed, opening up Birmingham to the rest of the country. Local places such as Dudley, Stourbridge, Coventry and Warwick were in easy reach, as well as further-afield places like London, Manchester, Liverpool and Bristol, and then the world.

But cutting these canals was not easy. The countryside around Birmingham consisted of many slopes and inclines, which meant the building of numerous locks. To get to Wednesbury it was necessary to build a flight of six locks. And because of the numerous locks that needed to be built between Birmingham and Worcester, it took twenty-four years to build this canal. It was completed on 21 July 1815, the same year the Worcester & Birmingham Canal Company built Lifford Reservoir.

With the opening of the Warwick Canal, which cut a corner off the Worcester Canal, hauliers such as Bird's, Whitehouse's, Robinson's and Crowley's were capable of reaching London a day sooner by avoiding the twelve locks along the Worcester Canal. There was a small charge per tonnage, but it was considered worth it, not least because it avoided any damage that could occur when going through the locks.

ROYAL DISAPPROVAL

On 21 October 1765, Edward, Duke of York had visited the town but had complained about the ballroom he danced in – he didn't like it. And it was probably because of this that the building of a new hotel was commissioned. In 1772, Wilday's Royal Hotel opened on Temple Row and its distinguished guests included Prince William of Gloucester, Lord Nelson, the Duke of Wellington and the King of France.

THE ASSAY OFFICE

In 1773, the Assay Office was established in Birmingham. Assay marks consist of the initials of the maker, the current king or queen's head, a letter depicting the year the item was made, the hallmark and the carat mark. For Birmingham, the hallmark is an anchor, which seems strange as Birmingham is so far from the coast – but hereby hangs a tale.

Prior to 1773, precious metal goods had to be taken to either London or Chester for assaying and hallmarking, but with the growth in Birmingham of this industry, manufacturers felt there was a desperate need for an assay office in Birmingham. Matthew Boulton was the leader in this feeling and through his friendship with Lord Dartmouth he was able to lobby Parliament.

On 28 May 1773, the Act was passed, and Birmingham could have its own assay office. It now came down to choosing the hallmark. While in London, Boulton stayed at the Crown and Anchor Inn and thought one of these would make an ideal hallmark. The toss of a coin decided that Birmingham's hallmark would be an anchor.

At first, the assaying was carried out once a week in rooms at the King's Head in New Street, then later in houses in Bull Street and Little Colmore Street. From 1816, an old Baptist church in Little Union Street was used before a purpose-built building was erected in 1877 in Newhall Street.

THEATRES

The Theatre Royal opened in 1774 on New Street and after an additional portico was added in 1780, with two busts over the attic windows depicting Shakespeare and Garrick, it was described as 'one of the most elegant theatres in Europe'. But it nearly came to a sudden end in 1792 due to a fire, which also destroyed all the scenery and costumes. Undeterred, its owners bought the adjoining buildings and four years later, it was larger and better. In 1807, it was given the name the Royal Theatre.

There had been a couple of theatres in Birmingham during the 1740s but they hadn't proved popular. The New Theatre was on Moor Street but that closed in 1752. Another two appeared on New Street and Smallbrook Street, but they too were short-lived.

Other theatres opened in the 1800s. The Royal Music Hall, with its impressive organ, which later became known as the Prince of Wales Theatre, opened in 1856 on Broad Street. More upper-class concerts were held here.

In the 1860s there was the New Theatre on Moor Street and the Empire Theatre, also known as Day's Music Hall, on the corner of Smallbrook Street and Hurst Street, which gave more

The New Theatre in Moor Street.

varied programmes. The Grand Theatre, the Queen's Theatre and the Imperial Theatre appeared in the 1880s and 1890s.

At the turn of the century, the Hippodrome and the Alexandra Theatres opened, and they have stood the test of time. Of course, there is also the Repertory Theatre, but we shall talk about that later.

A DOCTOR BUILDS A HOSPITAL

In 1766, work had begun on providing Birmingham with a General Hospital, but due to lack of funds it wasn't opened until 1778. Subscriptions had then been needed to complete the work, which cost £7,140. In 1790, two new wings were added.

For its upkeep, charity concerts were held every three years. Starting in 1784, they were held over a period of three days in October and became known as the Birmingham Music Festival. Morning concerts were held in St Philip's and evening concerts in the theatre.

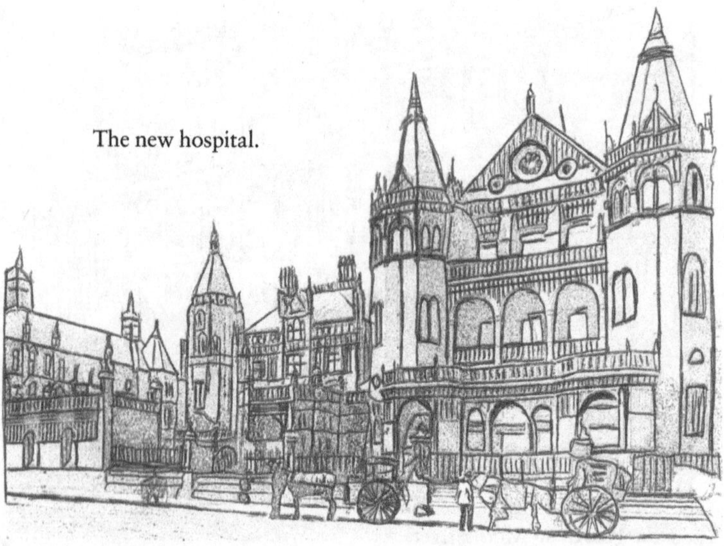

The new hospital.

The idea for the hospital had been nurtured by Dr John Ash. Born in 1723 in Coventry, the son of a brewer, he spent nine years between 1745 and 1754 studying at Trinity College in Oxford. Then he came to Birmingham, where he soon established a large surgery. He spent many years practising as a well-respected doctor at both his practice and the new hospital. In 1787, he moved to London and became a Fellow of the College of Physicians.

He originally lived at No. 9 Temple Row but acquired land from the Holte family and built a large house on the corner of Great Brook Street and Barrack Street. However, he never lived there as by the time it was completed he was moving to London. He gave the house to John Brooke, who then converted it into St James' Chapel. When the rest of the area was developed, it was given the name Ashted in the doctor's honour.

John Ash died in 1798.

FROM WIRES TO WEALTH

The Ryland family made their money in the wire-drawing trade, later manufacturing pins. In the late 1770s, John Ryland was to be found on the High Street as a wire drawer. His son Samuel was a pin maker on New Street. As their wealth increased, they progressed from being wealthy industrialists to the world of the landed gentry. John bought the property Easy Hill, which had once been the home of John Baskerville. He married wealthy heiress Martha Ruston in 1759 and they are immortalised in two Birmingham streets that lead off Broad Street.

Samuel Ryland passed the pin-making business to his nephew, Thomas Henry Phipson, and began to enjoy life as a gentleman. Thomas led the company into the 1800s as the leader in the pin industry. However, the 1842 Children's Employment Commission Report showed that Phipson's was the worst place for working children in Birmingham.

The workrooms were overcrowded, the 'privies' were dirty and the children were expected to work twelve or even fourteen hours a day. If they didn't, or didn't appear to be working hard enough, they would be lashed with a cane by the overseers.

A PLAYFUL WORKER

In 1780, James Pickard converted a corn mill at the bottom of Snow Hill to roll metal. On 23 August 1780, he patented a new idea. The first steam engines were worked by a rotary motion with an attached lever keeping the machinery working. Based on the Newcomen engine, Pickard's idea used the combination of a crank and flywheel with a lever attached to replace the pinions and racks used on the original machine. The lever was operated by a young boy. One day, this young boy wanted to play instead of work, so he fixed a pole from the engine to the lever of the pump, so that the engine supplied itself with water. When it was discovered, the boy wasn't reprimanded. Instead, his idea was developed and for his ingenuity, he was employed in a better position inside the mill.

GLASS FIT FOR A CHURCH

Francis Eginton had trained as an enameller in Bilston, Staffordshire, but in 1764 was taken on by Matthew Boulton. He quickly made a name for himself over the next few years and became a very skilled worker, particularly in the art of painting glass.

In 1784, setting up his own business, he began working from his home on Prospect Hill in Handsworth. From here, he produced many notable stained-glass windows for places such as St George's Chapel, Windsor, Salisbury and Lichfield Cathedrals, Tewkesbury Abbey, the east window of St Paul's,

Birmingham, the east window of the south aisle in St Peter and St Paul's Aston, and many more. His showroom opened its door to many visitors, including Lord Nelson.

He died in 1805, and his son William continued the business at his premises on Newhall Street. In 1816 he was appointed glass painter to Princess Charlotte.

A BOTANIST AND DOCTOR

Another doctor practising around the same time as John Ash was Dr William Withering. Born in Shropshire in 1741, he studied at Edinburgh University and as well as studying medicine he was also interested in collecting plants and botany. After qualifying, he set up a practice in Stafford but then, in May 1775, was invited by members of the Lunar Society to take over the practice of Dr William Small, Matthew Boulton's doctor, who had died. The practice went on to become the largest outside London.

His interest in plants led him to discover the presence of digitalis in foxgloves, a drug used in cardiac and circulatory problems. The story goes that it had come to his notice that a patient of his, who suffered from a severe heart condition and who he had been unable to treat, had improved significantly after taking a herbal remedy given to him by a gypsy. After searching for and finding her, he persuaded her to reveal the secret ingredient. Which was a purple foxglove. He began experimenting and found crushing the dried leaves gave excellent results. He introduced it officially in 1785 and it is still used in modern drugs today.

Withering lived at Edgbaston Hall for a time but then moved to The Larches in Ladypool as he preferred a smaller house. He died in 1799.

HOW TO UPSET A VICAR

In 1788, John Gough of Perry Hall built an inn on the Chester Road called the Royal Oak. It was also nicknamed the 'Parson and Clerk', due to two figures displayed on it. One was a vicar bowing his head in prayer and the other, a clerk, standing behind him with an axe as if he was going to chop off the vicar's head. They were put there by Gough to annoy the Reverend T. Lane, who he had been involved in a lawsuit with. Lane had withheld the licences for the inn, so Gough had sent his servants to church every day, thus forcing the Reverend Lane to hold a service every day.

BIRMINGHAM RIOTS

On Thursday, 14 June 1791, a dinner had been arranged at the Dadley Hotel in Temple Row. Tickets were 5*s* and on the day, eighty-one guests attended.

It may have been an innocent gathering of friends, but because those friends were wealthy Nonconformists who appeared to be celebrating Bastille Day, a small crowd of working-class men gathered outside the hotel to greet the guests with jeers and boos. On the whole, they remained calm, but as the crowd grew and drinks were passed around they became noisier. Somehow, an idea was installed in their heads that the people inside were planning an English revolution, and this incited the throng outside to start throwing stones and breaking the windows of the hotel. As the guests made their escape, they too were pelted with stones.

What followed were three days of devastation. As the numbers of rioters grew, they went on a rampage, destroying the houses and buildings of wealthy dissenters. The pulpit was ripped from Joseph Priestley's meeting house and the whole building set on fire. Others went to his house at

Fairview, 2 miles away, and before setting fire to that, they helped themselves to the wine in his cellar, becoming more intoxicated. John Ryland's house at Easy Hill was destroyed. Moseley Hall belonging to the Taylor family was also set alight. If the rioters were unable to set fire to a house because it wasn't a detached property, they dragged all the furniture and contents into the street and made a bonfire of those.

At first, extra constables had been sworn in and soldiers from the Oxford Blues had ridden to Birmingham, but by Sunday, reinforcements were needed and Elliot's Light Horse arrived from Nottingham. The majority of the rioters had scattered by Sunday evening and only a very small number of arrests were made. All but two of those were found not guilty at the Warwick Assizes on 23 August 1791. The two found guilty, Francis Field and John Green, were executed a few days later.

A POPULAR CAKE SHOP

Pattinson's was started by two maiden aunts in 1791. They sold buns and cakes to coach passengers in New Street. Situated on the left side of Corporation Street, with its prominent name board and 'witches hat'-style roof, it became known as the home of one of the best-known names in cakes and buns in Birmingham.

In 1888 the business became Pattinson and Co. Ltd Confectioners and moved into newly constructed buildings at Nos 25 & 27 Corporation Street. From here, they continued providing for the sweet-toothed population of Birmingham until the end of September 1967. By that time, the firm consisted of eighteen cake shops and restaurants, which employed 400 members of staff. Most of the branches were in Birmingham, but there were some in Sutton Coldfield, Solihull, Wolverhampton and Walsall.

ROYAL APPROVAL

Henry Clay started as an apprentice for John Baskerville but went on to become very successful on his own. He patented a stronger material than had previously been used in the panels on coaches and sedan chairs. In 1792, he presented Queen Charlotte with a sedan chair and after she gave her approval, he received many more orders from the elite. In 1803, he began to advertise himself as 'Japanner in Ordinary to His Majesty and his Royal Highness the Prince of Wales'.

He was now employing 300 workers at his New Hall Street premises and had introduced the use of bronze in his work. His own carriage, with a body of dark green and brown stripes and panels of papier-mâché, provided a superb advert for his work.

THE DISPENSARY

The Dispensary was a private establishment until Matthew Boulton became a patron in 1793. Situated in Temple Row, he took on the job as its treasurer and said that if at any time there were not enough funds he would make up the deficiency. In 1808, it moved to new premises in Union Street at a cost of around £3,000. Thousands received medical treatment there over the course of a year.

VISITORS TO BIRMINGHAM

On 2 September 1794, Edmund Hector died. He was a surgeon who had been practising in Birmingham for sixty-five years and was an old school friend of Dr Samuel Johnson.

Dr Johnson made many visits to Hector's house in the Old Square, but his father, Michael, had also been a regular visitor to Birmingham many years earlier. In the late 1600s there were no bookshops in the town and Michael Johnson came to Birmingham from Lichfield on market days to set up his stall to sell books.

FROM BUCKLES TO BUTTONS

By the 1780s the buckle industry was a large industry in Birmingham with an estimated 4,000 workers being employed in the trade. But in the early 1790s the shoelace was introduced, and shoe buckles became less popular. Fearing for their livelihoods, buckle-makers petitioned the king and some even travelled to London to seek an audience with him. At first, everything seemed to be going their way when he promised he and his household would continue to use buckles. But the reprise was short-lived and buckles did go out of fashion. However, help was on hand because as buckles lost their appeal, buttons were becoming more fashionable, and many of the buckle-makers transferred to a new industry.

Buttons were first made in Birmingham in 1689, when they were described as 'oval chucks'. But by the late 1700s and early 1800s they were all shapes and sizes – square, round, oval, pyramid, even pea-like. They were also made in different materials – brass, pearl, glass, porcelain, bone, iron, leather, papier-mâché and gilded metals. The prices differed too, from threepence a gross to as much as 140 guineas. The expensive ones were made of highly polished steel and looked like diamonds.

A JOB FOR THE HEIR HUNTERS

In 1798, William Jennens, who was a bachelor, died aged 98 at Acton in Suffolk (although some records suggest he was 103). His estate was worth around £1 million, but the income from that was said to put the whole estate nearer to £2 million.

However, there was a problem, he died intestate because on the day he was supposed to have signed his will, he had forgotten his glasses. William was the great-grandson of John Jennens, the Birmingham iron manufacturer, and grandson of Humphrey Jennens, but had no immediate family.

At first, the Court of Chancery approved George Curzon, a descendant of his aunt, Hester Jennens, to be his heir but when George died, his mother, as administrator, transferred the estate to her other son, Richard Curzon. However, this was disputed due to an allegation that Richard wasn't actually George's brother, but the illegitimate son of a single woman who had been adopted by the Curzon family.

Lady Mary Andover, a great-granddaughter of Humphrey Jennens, and William Lygon, Earl Beauchamp and grandson of Hester Jennens, now claimed to be his nearest relations, and the courts agreed. But were they?

Over the decades that followed, numerous other claimants came forward, all descended from the Jennens family. Clubs were even formed of people who thought they were descendants of Humphrey Jennens. These clubs existed in many different places, from Birmingham to Ireland, and members hired genealogists to prove their entitlement. In fact, the case became so well known, Charles Dickens based the story of Jarndyce v Jarndyce in *Bleak House* on the case.

The last claim failed in 1915. But even in 1930, the case was still rumbling. A document dated February 1826 was found in a vault in Melbourne. However, nothing more seems to have happened with this claim.

THE SAILOR'S RETURN

In 1798, the son of Dr Spencer, the Vicar of Aston, was killed in the Battle of the Nile. The young officer survived long enough to give his watch and a few other small items to John Parkes, a sailor under his command, to take back to his father.

It was some years before Parkes was able to do so and in the course of time, he had lost a leg in another battle. But he eventually reached Aston and the Reverend Dr Spencer. The father was so pleased to receive his only son's effects that he asked the old sailor what he could give him. Parkes told him that he had always wanted his own pub. Dr Spencer obliged and the public house on the corner of Watery Lane and Lawley Street was given the name The Sailor's Return.

THE APPRENTICE

The largest man known at the time died in June 1809. He was aged 39 and, measuring 9ft around his body, he weighed 52st 11lb. On coming to Birmingham as boy, he was taken on as an apprentice to John Taylor, a button maker of Crooked Lane. However, during his time there he became so fat his indentures were cancelled, and he was sent back to his father in Leicester.

AT THE BEGINNING OF THE 1800S

Despite developing into an industrial town, Birmingham still had a countryside atmosphere. At Smithfield, south of St Martin's Church, cattle, sheep and pigs were still sold. The house that had been built in 1730 to replace the manor house was still surrounded by a moat, although in 1816 the moat was filled in and the site converted into a marketplace. By 1851, the place where the house had once stood was known as Moat Row.

There were still many half-timbered buildings in the Bull Ring and cows grazing where the Town Hall now stands in Victoria Square. The Old Square was a quadrangle of elegant houses with a central garden of lawns, shrubs and flowers, all surrounded by iron railings.

The early 1800s brought about more improvements to Birmingham. The houses around St Martin's were demolished and the area was turned into Market Place, with the streets widened and repaved. Market Cross was erected here, from where the miles to Birmingham were measured.

In 1806, the new Public Office was built in Moor Street. Costing £9,000, it housed the Street Commissioners on the ground floor and the magistrates on the upper floor. At the back were the apartments for the prison keeper and his attendants. The prison itself was split into two parts by a lofty brick wall – men on one side and women on the other.

The roads around Birmingham from other places were not in a good condition. From the effects of rain and constant use, and with no repairs being undertaken, they were hollowed.

In some places, they were lower in the middle than by the footpath. But the trustees of the turnpikes organised repairs on them and soon they were as good as new.

There were three hotels for upper-class travellers, where they could find rooms not just for themselves, but for their horses and carriages too. The Royal Hotel was close to St Philip's and the Duke of Gloucester stayed there on 4 May 1805. There was also the Swan Hotel on the High Street and the Hen and Chickens Hotel on New Street. For the less wealthy there were taverns and inns, including the Stork, in the Square; the Nelson, opposite the statue in Market Place; the Union, on Union Street; the Saracen's Head, on Bull Street; the George and the Castle on the High Street; and the Wool Pack on Moor Street. In Digbeth, there was the White Hart, and in Edgbaston, the Rose.

Industry was booming, with Birmingham metal and iron workers making anything and everything. There was also brass-working, gun-making, plating and japanning. Birmingham entered the nineteenth century with its head held high.

THE TURN OF THE SCREW

Edward Thomason began working as an apprentice at the Soho Works in 1785 when he was 16. His father was a reputable buckle-maker with a shop on the corner of Colmore Row and Church Street. It was said he made 1,000 pairs of buckles per day. One design, which he called the Silver Penny, gave him a profit of £1,000.

When he died in 1793, Edward took over his business and, like many buckle-makers following the decline in the buckle industry, turned to making buttons. He also made coins and medals but, becoming a pioneer in plating, he added silver spoons, sugar tongs and wine bottle labels, among similar things, to his catalogue and became very successful.

Over the years his factory was extended and eventually consisted of about sixty workrooms. There were also twelve showrooms, which were visited by many important people from all over the country and even the world. One item Thomason was well known for was the corkscrew, which he patented in 1802 and sold over 250,000 in the first years of manufacture.

Thomason was knighted in 1832 and retired in 1844. During his retirement, he moved to Ludlow, then Bath and finally Warwick, where he died in 1849.

THE TOOL SHOP

Richard Timmins started his business in 1792 in Hurst Street and manufactured all sorts of steel tools. In 1821, his three sons joined him and the business known as Timmins & Sons grew. Then in 1851, having accumulated several shops and warehouses in Hurst Street, they moved to Pershore Street.

The last of the sons, Samuel, died in 1887 and the business was bought by Wynn & Co., who specialised in adjustable spanners and wrenches. Wynn & Co. had begun as edge-toolmakers in 1813 on Exeter Row, Suffolk Street. In 1872, they had moved to Commercial Street. The company now became known as Wynn, Timmins & Co. and continued as toolmakers until 1969.

A SCHOOL LIKE NO OTHER

Thomas Wright Hill was born in Kidderminster in 1763 and at first became a brass founder, having been apprenticed at the age of 14 in Birmingham. But he became interested in education and more intellectual pursuits – in particular, astronomy – and became a Fellow of the Royal Astronomical Society and a member of Matthew Boulton's Lunar Society.

In 1802, he took over a boys' school on Lionel Street and moved it to Gough Street before having a new building built on the Hagley Road in Edgbaston. Named Hazelwood, he wanted his school to be unique and exciting for pupils and their studies to be enjoyable. He even allowed the boys to form their own committees and make their own rules.

In 1827, Hill moved to Tottenham in London and the school moved with him. Hazelwood then became a private residence.

Thomas was also the father of a famous son who spent some time teaching at Hazelwood. Later, Roland Hill went on to introduce the postal system as we know it today.

GO DIRECTLY TO GAOL

In 1802, one of the worst prisons in England was said to be Bordesley Prison, also known as Tarte's Hole, the name of one of its keepers. It serviced the parish of Aston. Situated at the back of the keeper's house, it had two damp and dark dungeons that measured 12ft by 7ft. The only entrance was through a trapdoor and ten steps. There was a small iron-grated opening of 1ft square, which the light came through. Very often there was an inch of water trickling around the floor. There were two other cells in the yard measuring 12ft each. These were used for those who had committed petty crimes, such as apprentices who had run away and servants who had been disobedient.

The Debtors' Prison was in a small courtyard in Philip Street. Just one damp dungeon measuring 10ft by 11ft, it was accessed by a flight of seven steps. Sometimes, up to fifteen people, men and women, were held in this cell. However, it did have an extra room above, of the same size, for sleeping in.

THE START OF THE CHOCOLATE DYNASTY

When Richard Tapper Cadbury arrived in Birmingham, he was to start a dynasty that is still around today. He had been born in Exeter on 6 November 1768 and came to Birmingham in 1794, after serving as a draper's apprentice in Gloucester. On arriving he started his own drapery business.

He married Elizabeth Head in 1796, and the family eventually consisted of five sons and five daughters. At first, they lived in the Old Square, then they moved to No. 92 Bull Street in 1800. He adapted the house to include a shop for his business and many beautiful lengths of silk material draped over tall Oriental vases were displayed in the windows. At one end of his shop, a corner was curtained off, and it was here that customers were invited to sit and have a drink. It was not an alcoholic one though – with the introduction of the temperance movement, Richard was among the first to take the pledge. When ladies began to wear huge gigot sleeves stuffed with feather pillows, Richard had to have the shop door widened for them to be able to get in.

By 1832, Richard had retired and moved out to the countryside. His new address was No. 58 Calthorpe Road, Edgbaston, which now forms part of the massive Five Ways road junction. He died in March 1860, leaving behind his children and a total of forty grandchildren and great-grandchildren. He was buried in the Society of Friends Cemetery in Bull Street and as a mark of respect due to him being one of the principal traders in Birmingham for many years, the shops along Bull Street were closed as the funeral procession passed through. But his drapery business no longer existed. The name Cadbury was now synonymous with chocolate, as will be told later.

HORSE SALES

In the early 1800s, if you wanted to buy or sell a horse there was only one place to go, the Repository on Cheapside, owned by John Beardsworth. John had begun life as a hackney coach driver. The story of how he made his money may be true or just a legend, but it tells that one night he took a young heiress to a ball. Totally enamoured by her, he rushed home and got changed. Somehow, he managed to gain entry to the ball, where he danced with her and eventually married her. With her monies he was able to amass a small fortune, nearly a quarter of a million, and with this built the Repository, together with a house furnished with the best money could buy. One notable item was a centre table made of rare wood from America that cost £1,500 – a lot of money in those days.

Unfortunately, he was a gambling man and lost a small fortune betting at the races. But in 1830, at the Doncaster St Leger, his horse called Birmingham came first out of twenty-seven others. He won £40,000 and gave the jockey, Connelly, £2,000.

He died in 1838, with his wife Caroline having died a few years earlier.

NEW CHURCHES

By the early 1800s Birmingham was a place of many religions. A chapel for Catholics had been erected in Broad Street in 1789 and then renovated in 1800, and a new meeting house for the Society of Friends was erected in Bull Street. The old meeting house for Dissenters had been destroyed by fire in 1791, so a new one was erected in 1793 with an organ that was said to be 'suitable for the size of the building'.

Calvinists had a meeting house in Carrs Lane, but they also converted a riding school in Livery Street, and on 9 December 1818 opened a new meeting house along Steelhouse Lane.

This one was fitted with pews and could hold a congregation of 2,000. It was also lit by gas.

The Methodists had a chapel in Cherry Street, which had been erected in 1782 and had been opened by John Wesley. Others were situated in Belmont Row, Bradford Street and Oxford Street.

A Baptist chapel was erected on Canon Street in 1804, followed by ones in Newhall Street, Bond Street and Lombard Street, Deritend. The followers of Lady Huntingdon used what was formerly a theatre in King Street, while the Swedenborgians had their New Jerusalem Temple in Newhall Street and there was a Jewish synagogue in Severn Street.

CHARITABLE WAYS

The Birmingham of the early 1800s became a place where the poor were helped in many ways, although some charities had been founded in the 1700s. George Fentham, a Birmingham mercer, set up the Fentham's Trust to help educate poor children and clothe poor widows. He bequeathed £100 per annum for the children to be taught at the Blue Coat School. They were distinguishable from the other children as they wore green. In 1733, Mrs Crowley had left six houses in trust to support ten girls who were also at the Blue Coat School.

A society was formed in 1800 by a group of unnamed ladies to provide clothing for destitute women and children. The Cadbury family may have been involved as notices said subscriptions and donations were to be handed in at Mr Cadbury's on Bull Street. The subscriptions were 3*s* and 5*s* per quarter and would help around 400 people.

The Female Benevolent Society was set up in 1802 to help married women during childbirth or any womanly illness. To qualify, the woman would be visited by two officials who would analyse her situation. She could then receive anything from 5–10*s* during her illness or confinement. Poor widows could receive 9*d* per week over a three-month period. During the first nine years, £417 16*s* was distributed. Mrs Dickson of Summer Hill collected the subscriptions and donations.

Set up around 1803, the Depositing Society improved the condition of the poor by encouraging them to save money for a rainy day. A committee consisting of ladies only, although the treasurer was a Mr J. Dickenson of Summer Hill, allowed small premiums on every shilling deposited. So, if they fell on hard times, the poor then had money to buy coal, clothes, bedding and such-like, as well as help to pay debts and redeem pledges.

In 1806, the Deritend and Bordesley Society helped provide sick children with clean linen. The society comprised six visitors, a treasurer and storekeeper. Those who needed help had to provide a letter of proof and then a visitor would go and assess the situation and put in an order for what they considered necessary.

An institute for providing clothes for newborn infants was introduced in 1814 to raise funds to purchase linen, flannels and other supplies. The subscription was 2*s* 6*d,* but if the subscriber paid more they could then recommend a family.

The Lying-in Charity at Five Ways asked for voluntary contributions of either money or goods. The object was to supply poor, married women with linen during their confinement and provide them with a set of linen for their baby.

In 1526 William Lench, a tanner on Moor Street, had bequeathed land at the bottom of Steelhouse Lane to build almshouses. Known as Lench's Trust, by the 1800s there were twelve almshouses at the bottom of Steelhouse Lane, nine others in Dudley Street and four in Park Street. They were large enough to accommodate fifty-two elderly ladies, who were cared for by sixteen trustees. At the beginning of the twenty-first century, 200 elderly people were being looked after by the trust.

GLASS LIGHTS

Glass had been manufactured in Birmingham since the latter half of the 1700s by Meyer Oppenheim, who had set up a glass house on Snow Hill in 1762. The business mainly supplied the raw materials to other trades until the end of the eighteenth century.

In 1807, Thomas Osler set up a business in Broad Street making small trinkets and, later, chandeliers. He became very successful and made some of the most beautiful chandeliers, fountains and tableware of his day. Osler's was well-known around the world for its unique and beautiful glassware and eventually expanded to having a branch in London at No. 44 Oxford Street. In 1919, Osler joined forces with the lighting company Faraday & Sons and, as Osler & Faraday Ltd, remained in business until 1965.

After they had closed, a workshop manager took charge of some of their patterns and made a few items for private orders. When he died in 1985, these patterns and drawings were bought by Wilkinsons, who registered them under the name of Osler & Faraday to keep the heritage of the old company going.

A CELEBRATED STATUE

Following Nelson's visit, and after he had said how much he liked Birmingham, a statue was erected at the top of Market Place in front of St Martin's Church to honour him. Erected on 24 October 1809, it was made possible by public subscriptions of £2,500 collected by a Mr Westmacott. The Earl of Dudley donated the largest amount, giving £150. The smallest donations were the pennies given by workers who had clubbed together. For many years, it was a meeting place for gatherings and annual parades.

A statue standing proud.

Made of bronze by Elkington & Mason of Newhall Street, it was the second erected in the world, the first one being in Montreal. Although that one, being made of stone, had to be replaced in the 1980s. So now Birmingham's statue is the oldest surviving public statue of Nelson in the world.

FIRST DAYS AT SCHOOL

The National School was erected in Pinfold Street in 1810, and its lofty brick walls enclosed separate playgrounds for boys and girls. Also separated inside, the boys were educated on the ground floor, where there was enough room to accommodate 500 pupils, and the upper level provided schooling for 400 girls.

The classes were based on the Madras system, which had been invented by Dr Andrew Bell. The older or brighter children were taught and then they passed on what they had learnt to the younger or less-intelligent children. Only children belonging to the Church of England were educated there.

A Protestant Dissenters' Charity School could be found in Park Street, although only girls were admitted. The boys could be educated at a boys' school called the Royal Lancastrian Free School in Severn Street. Built in 1800, all dominations were accepted and up to 400 boys could be accommodated. Exams took place every Saturday.

For one penny a week, Sunday schools could be found in every part of the town and were well attended by children of Church of England families. Dissenters had their own Sunday schools.

TWICE EXECUTED

In February 1812, suspicions were aroused surrounding William Booth, who rented a 200-acre farm in Perry Barr, and plans were made to search the property. A search warrant was issued and Joseph Chirm, the headborough of Birmingham, swore in ten extra constables and enlisted the help of seven Dragoon guards.

On 16 March 1812, they made their way to the property but rather foolishly stopped off at the Boar's Head in Perry Barr. Dorothy Ingeley, a member of the Booth family, spotted them and rushed to the farm to warn the occupants. When the search party arrived, they found the farmhouse laid out like a fortress. The entrance of the house was secured by three doors with numerous locks and bolts and the shutters on the windows were also bolted.

However, they managed to force their way through an upstairs window just in time to witness William Booth removing blank pieces of paper that were very similar in size to bank notes. Inside the room, they found numerous pieces of equipment and machinery that had been used for forging both banknotes and coins. The entrance doors to this and an adjoining room had been bricked up and the only way out was through a trapdoor, also securely locked, which opened out through the ceiling of the parlour.

After arresting Booth, whose hands were very dirty from what appeared to be printing ink, the constables spent a week searching the house, outbuildings and surrounding fields, where they found further evidence relating to his forgery exploits. At the Summer Assizes in Stafford, he was found guilty and sentenced to death.

His execution took place on 12 August. However, as the drop was released, the rope slipped from the tree and he fell from the gallows some 8 or 10ft. He was revived and then spent two hours waiting for the gallows to be repaired.

A song was later written about him entitled 'Twice Tried, Twice Hung, Twice Buried'. Twice tried because he had previously been in court accused of murdering his brother, for which he had been acquitted due to insufficient evidence. And twice buried because following boundary changes between Birmingham and Staffordshire, his body was exhumed and buried in St Mary's in Handsworth to put him back in the correct county.

The farmhouse was later demolished in the twentieth century when the area was being developed for new housing, and even up to the 1950s coins made by Booth were still being found in the gardens of those houses.

FOR PUBLIC SAFETY

On 4 October 1813, the foundations for a Proof House were laid on the banks of the canal along Banbury Street. When completed, a plaque over the door said that it had been 'established for public safety'.

Previously, the inspection of guns had taken place in a building in Bagot Street, where a group of inspectors visually inspected the guns for any signs of faults. An Act of Parliament now changed this very basic procedure to include firing the gun, using overloaded cartridges, in a safe room in the building. This procedure exposed the gun to a pressure that wouldn't normally happen. If no damage was caused to the gun, it was therefore considered safe to use and given a stamp of approval. Larger guns were tested on a shooting range out at Bordesley.

WHERE TO BURY THE DEAD

Up to the early 1800s, burials took place on consecrated land attached to the church, known commonly as churchyards. However, with them now being quite full, an alternative had to be found.

In 1807, St Martin's Church bought a piece of ground on Park Street for £1,600. The ground was then levelled and fenced off with appropriate walls and railings at a cost of £764. Consecrated on 16 July 1813, it became Birmingham's first cemetery. Sadly, it later became a victim of the new railway, with a line ploughing right through it. Uncared for and no longer in use, it was eventually taken on by the Corporation in 1878 and turned into a children's park.

Twenty years after Birmingham's first cemetery was consecrated, with the ever-increasing rise in population, a meeting was held on 18 October 1832 to investigate developing more cemeteries. Following this, the old sandpits at Icknield Street were bought and the 12-acre site became Key Hill Cemetery, which opened specifically for Nonconformists to have their own burial ground.

The Birmingham Church of England Cemetery Company was formed and another 15 acres of disused sandpits were purchased. Warstone Lane Cemetery was consecrated on 20 August 1848.

There then followed the development of a larger cemetery on Moor Lane and, covering 150 acres, Witton Cemetery was opened in 1863 and went on to become known as the City Cemetery.

Five more cemeteries were developed on the outskirts of Birmingham: Sutton Coldfield in 1881; South Yardley in 1883; Lodge Hill, Selly Oak, in 1895; Brandwood End, King's Heath, in 1899; and Handsworth in 1909.

THE NOT SO GOOD YEARS

Following the Napoleonic Wars, the country showed signs of financial difficulties, social conflict and a slump in trade. Birmingham felt the strain too. In fact, trade was so bad that the workhouse was stretched to its limits. At the time, it was run by twelve overseers and 108 Guardians.

Help was needed, and therefore it was necessary to ask for donations. An amazing amount of £60,214 17*s* 6*d* was collected. The following year, £15,943 9*s* 9*d* was given. Both of these were staggering amounts for the times.

THE END OF AN ERA

The year 1818 saw the last descendant of the Holte family leave Aston Hall. Sir Lister Holte, the 5th Baronet, had married three times but had no children. So, when he died in 1770, his brother, Sir Charles succeeded. He never lived at Aston Hall. His wife and Lister's widow didn't get on and were always arguing, so for a time the head of the Holte family lived at Erdington Hall.

Sir Charles died on 12 March 1782 at his London home in Portland Square, leaving just one daughter. With him, the title and the Holte line died, and unfortunately so did the family fortunes.

Mary Elizabeth Holte married Abraham Bracebridge on 12 September 1775 at St Michael's in Lichfield, and on her father's death she inherited the large estate. On the strength of this, Abraham used it as security on the establishment, patenting and manufacturing of a soap. However, the business proved unsuccessful and he lost a large amount of money.

In April 1818, Aston Hall was put up for sale and bought by Greenway, Greaves & Whitehead, bankers of Warwick. Later in the year, it was advertised as being available for rent and was taken up by James Watt Jnr, who lived there until his death in 1848.

Aston Hall.

By now, the area had begun to change. The estate had been reduced to 370 acres, a new street ploughed its way through the park and houses were being built. But rescue did come, as will be seen later.

Christmas Eve in Aston Hall

A tradition that was held for several years at Aston Hall took place on Christmas Eve. Once supper was over, the table was cleared, and a loaf of bread placed on it. On top of the loaf there were then placed twenty silver threepenny bits. Seated at the table were the two oldest servants. The other servants were brought in one at a time by the steward, each covered with a curtain. They put their right hands on the loaf to just expose the backs of their hands. The two older servants then guessed who the hand belonged to. If they were correct, the servant was taken back to their quarters. If the guess was incorrect, the servant was taken to sit on the window ledge and given one of the silver coins. This continued until all the money had been won. Once the game was over, the servants were then allowed to drink, dance and be merry.

THROWING DOWN THE GAUNTLET

In 1818, a court case took place that was going to take many months to resolve and also involve Parliament.

On 27 May 1817, the body of Mary Ashford was found in a pit in Penn Mills. It appeared that she had been raped and murdered. The night before, she had been to a dance at Tyburn, where she had been seen in the company of Abraham Thornton and they had been seen leaving together. He was immediately arrested but insisted that he was innocent of her murder, although he admitted to having been intimate with her but with her consent. At his trial, the defence produced witnesses who said they had seen Abraham at certain times at distances too far from Penn Mills for him to have committed the murder. It was also suggested that, feeling ashamed of what she had allowed Abraham to do to her, Mary committed suicide by jumping in the pit, even though there were footprints on the edge of the pit suggesting she had been thrown in.

When Abraham was found not guilty, Mary's brother, William, called for an 'Appeal of Murder', an old law where the next of kin could request a second trial. That trial took place six months later and on being asked how he pleaded, Abraham said, 'Not guilty and I am ready to defend the same with my life'. Whereupon he threw a gauntlet to the floor demanding a trial by combat.

This was another old law that hadn't been heard of for 200 years. It meant that William Ashford would have to fight with Abraham until one of them was dead or had given up. If Abraham won, he would go free, if William won, Abraham would be hanged immediately.

There now followed months of debates in court while it was decided if this was still legal. In the end, it was decided that this old law had never been repealed by Parliament, so therefore it was. William refused to fight with Abraham, so Abraham went free, and an Act of Parliament removed this old law from existence.

CUPS AND MEDALS

In 1819, Philip Vaughton, a goldsmith and jeweller, set up a shop in Little Hampton Street that was described as a gold and seal makers. Over the years, Philip Vaughton & Son moved around a bit, although not far, always staying in the vicinity of Great Hampton Street. Then in 1902, they moved into a purpose-built factory named Vaughton's Gothic Works in Livery Street and became known as Vaughtons Ltd.

By now they had become celebratory manufacturers of tokens, medals and such-like. They made the FA Cup, which was used between 1895 and 1910, and the medals for the 1908 Olympic Games.

Although it is no longer a family business, the company still exists at No. 16 Well Street, Birmingham, having amalgamated with W.H. Darby in 1994. But their old factory in Livery Street is still standing and has become a Grade 2 listed building.

A TINY LADY STAYS IN BIRMINGHAM

On 4 May 1819, Nanetta Stocker died aged 39. Known as the smallest woman in Britain, she measured a mere 33in tall.

She had been born in Austria and, as was normal in those days, she knew that because of her height she could earn a living by 'exhibiting' herself. She met John Hauptman who, at 3ft 6in, was taller than her, and they formed a double act. She played the piano and he played the violin. They would also dance together.

Travelling across Europe, they eventually came to Birmingham, where she was a triumph. It was while performing there that she died and was buried in the grounds of St Philip's, very near to the west door.

WHERE THERE'S BRASS

Robert Winfield set up his brass foundry in Cambridge Street in 1820. His family had lived in Leicestershire for many generations, and it was his grandfather Edward who moved to Birmingham in the mid-1700s. Robert was born in 1799 at Davenport House on the Hagley Road and his first job was with a jeweller and toymaker by the name of Benjamin Cooke.

From starting in a very small way, it became one of the largest businesses at the time, employing 400 workers. Determined to be a success, he knew the only way to achieve this was to have high-quality tools and machinery and employ the best workers. And the only way to get the best workers was to pay the best wages.

His ideals certainly worked for him as he soon had a reputation of providing excellently designed goods that were exported all over the world. And as his business grew, so did his factory. As various extensions were added to the existing building, his site eventually covered numerous acres, with some parts of the factory rising five or six storeys high. He also bought the Union Rolling Mill near his factory to produce rolled metals of all sorts.

Winfield was one of the first to apply the stamping and lacquering process to his products to produce the unique colour that was greatly admired. Soon he was producing almost everything that was made of brass, copper and tin – tubes, gas fittings, chandeliers, curtain rods, picture frames, umbrella stands, bedsteads, ships' fittings and ornamental metal work. He made every type of bed – from the basic ones used by the workhouse, asylums and other institutes to elaborate and ornate four-posters.

In 1853, he created what was said to be the most beautiful brass chandelier of its day. It was designed in the Italian style and decorated in a most ornate way, which included masks and figurines of peace, plenty and love. He sent it to Osborne

House and Prince Albert said it was the most beautiful piece he had ever seen.

A pioneer of compulsory education, Winfield provided evening classes for the boys who worked for him and a large room was especially built for the purpose. They had no choice, they had to attend. Then, once a year, in May, he would hold a fete in his gardens and invite all his students. And at Christmas, he distributed prizes and certificates of achievement in the school room.

His only son, John, helped with some of the classes but he unfortunately died suddenly in January 1861, aged 37. This came as a great shock to his father, who never really got over it.

He lived at the Hawthorns on Ladywood Road, which he had had built in 1828, and in later life was considered quite old-fashioned. His clothes were made of black broadcloth, and he wore a stiff beaver hat, a starched white cravat for a tie, and his coat resembled that of the type worn fifty years earlier. He died on 16 December 1869.

PENS GALORE

Joseph Gillott was born in Sheffield in 1799 into a very poor family and from an early age was sent out to work to help with the household's finances. He was taken on as an apprentice, forging and grinding the blades of penknives and scissors. It was said he was very accurate and excelled in his work, even up against older, more experienced workers. When his apprenticeship finished, he decided to come to Birmingham, where he found work making metal buckles for shoes and belts. Again, he proved successful, so he decided to branch out on his own and took a house in Bread Street (later named Cornwall Street).

Soon the steel pen industry was taking off and Joseph met the sister of two penmakers called William and John Mitchell. While courting Maria, he watched her brothers laboriously making each pen individually and thought that the presses he was using to make buckles could be adjusted to make pens. He experimented with the idea – and on the morning he married Maria, 15 September 1823, he made 144 of them and sold them at a shilling each to his wedding guests. He was soon making the same number of pens single-handed that twenty workers would have made.

Within a short time, he was becoming a very wealthy man. In 1828, he moved to larger premises in Church Street and then in 1833 progressed to larger premises in Newhall Street. Of course, by now, he was employing workers to help with the demand and in 1836 records show that he had produced 36 million pens. His last move was to a large factory in Graham Street that had been built between 1838 and 1840.

Joseph Gillott became a millionaire, and this resulted in him becoming a great collector of what he considered beautiful things. He collected precious stones, in particular, rare ones. He also collected string instruments and had a collection of violins that, after his death in 1873, were sold at auction for £4,000. Visiting gardens in Leamington one day, he spotted a tree he liked and asked how much it was. Being told it wasn't for sale, he insisted he wanted it and said he would pay £100 for it – which he did. He also collected art and was a good friend of Joseph Turner, purchasing numerous of his paintings. His collection was the largest in private hands, and after his death, it sold for five times the amount he had paid for it.

THE FIRST MEDICAL SCHOOL IN BIRMINGHAM

In 1828, William Sands Cox, who was a surgeon in Birmingham, announced in local newspapers that he was going to start a course of lectures and demonstrations at No. 24 Temple Street. Three years later, his idea was expanded into the formation of a medical school.

The Birmingham Medical School was founded in 1834 and integrated into the General Hospital. On 18 June 1840, the first stone was laid by Earl Howe for the new Queen's Hospital and College on Bath Row.

THE TOWN HALL

The Birmingham music festival was still taking place every three years, but by the 1820s, having become very popular, a larger venue was needed. Work on Birmingham Town Hall began in 1828, and it was ready for opening in 1834, although construction continued and it wasn't officially completed until 1850. The cost had been estimated at between £17,000 and £19,000, but with all the alterations that had been made during those twenty-two years, it eventually cost £69,520.

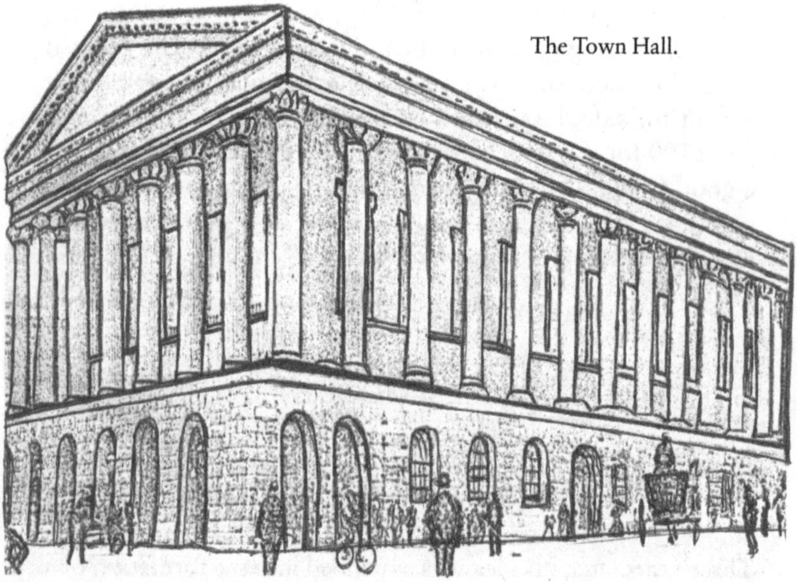

The Town Hall.

Described as being the 'finest specimen of architecture in the town and the finest music hall in the country', it housed a 6,000-pipe organ and over the years, many celebrities, musicians, even politicians have performed or given speeches there. It closed for ten years in 1996 for refurbishment then reopened with a two-week festival, celebrating the old and the new.

A BEAUTIFUL GARDEN

In 1829, as a nationwide interest in foreign and tropical plants became popular, the Birmingham Botanical and Horticultural Society was formed. With an initial subscription of £2,000, it acquired 12 acres of land on the Calthorpe estate in Edgbaston. Known as Holly Bank Farm, the farm had originally been leased to an insurance broker who had enjoyed farming as a hobby and looked on it as a bit of fun. Three years later, that farmland had become the Botanical Gardens.

Opening on 11 July 1832, the gardens consisted of ornamental conservatories, lawns, herbaceous beds and an arboretum. But the glasshouses were the main attraction and were extended over the years. When the gardens first opened, subscribers and shareholders were given free admission and

Glass houses in the Botanical Gardens.

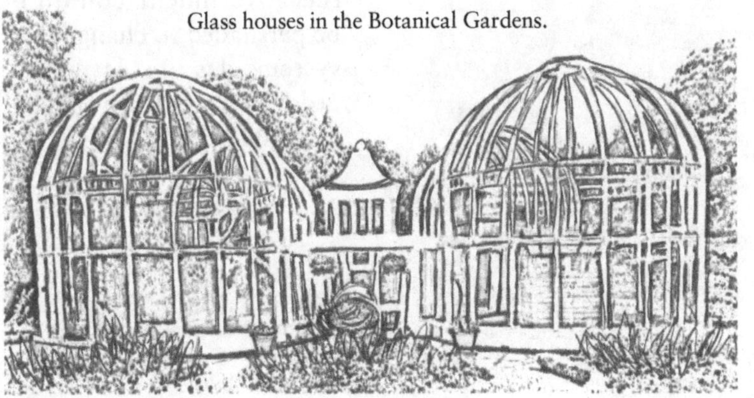

could take four members of their family with them. General admission was 1*s* per person and 6*d* for the under 10s. But on Mondays, the gardens were opened to the working classes for just one penny per person.

In 1852, a tropical house was built, in 1871, the subtropical house followed, and in 1884 the original conservatories were replaced with terraced glasshouses. A bandstand was built in 1873. Numerous functions have been held in the gardens and buildings since 1832, including flower shows, wedding receptions, music and play festivals, even political meetings.

GOLD OR PAPER AND THE WORKING MAN

Thomas Attwood was born in Halesowen in 1783, the son of a wealthy iron manufacturer, and moved to Birmingham around 1800 to work in the bank his father also owned. Working alongside local industrialists and businessmen, he realised there was a necessity for reform in British currency. His Birmingham contemporaries liked his ideas of changing from gold coins to paper money for general use, which he felt would help the economy immensely, but the government couldn't be persuaded to change the system, despite Attwood producing a petition signed by 40,000 people.

A statue of Thomas Attwood lounging on the steps in Chamberlain Square.

In 1829, the Birmingham Political Union began to take shape, and Attwood became its leader following a speech made at a meeting of around 10,000 people in January 1830. Then, following two years of campaigning, the Reform Bill of 1832, which gave more people the right to vote, was passed. But with a £10 rental qualification, there were still a large number who weren't entitled to vote.

With the new reforms, the general election on 10 December 1832 allowed Thomas Attwood to enter the Houses of Parliament as Birmingham's first MP. Although he didn't approve of the aggressive ways some Chartists adopted, he continued to fight for the rights of the working classes.

His life as an MP was short-lived, however. He became increasingly frustrated at the government's approach to reform, so when a national petition of 1,280,000 signatures was rejected in 1839, he resigned and concentrated on his banking career. He lived at The Grove in Harborne, which is now a park known as Grove Park, between 1823 and 1846, but he was living in Great Malvern when he died in 1856.

A MIXTURE OF METALS

George Frederick Muntz came from a family who had originally belonged to Polish aristocracy but had been living in France for generations. His father, Philip Frederick, was a merchant who left France at the start of the revolution and found his way via Amsterdam to England, and then Birmingham.

At the age of 41, Philip married Catherine Purden on 6 March 1793. She was aged 17. George was born in November 1794 and Catherine, who was an intelligent young lady, took great pains to give her young son an early education at home, before moving him to the school of Dr Currie in Small Heath.

Philip died in 1811, which left the young George, as the eldest son, in charge of two businesses – a rolling mill in Water

Street and a merchant's business in Great Charles Street. He proved successful in business, but a lucky discovery took him even higher up the business scale. By mixing sixteen parts of copper with ten and two thirds spelter, a metal was produced that proved equally as good for sheathing ships' bottoms as copper on its own but was a lot cheaper. Leaving the running of the family's two businesses to his younger brother, he concentrated on the making of Muntz metal.

Muntz rolling machines were made of smooth iron cylinders and as a worker threaded a piece of metal through, it was pressed to the desired thickness, then removed at the other end by another worker. The sheets were then annealed to harden them and make them more brittle. In 1844, after 400 ships in the London Docks had been fitted with Muntz metal, Liverpool ship owners and others from elsewhere began placing orders.

George married the daughter of a clergyman, and the couple had a large family. But business was not his only passion – he soon started looking towards politics, where he would make his mark in Victorian Birmingham.

PAPER MILLS

James Baldwin first started working in Newhall Street but in 1829 he established a paper mill in Morville Street, Ladywood. Later, in 1835, he established one on Lifford Lane, King's Norton, named Sherborne Mill. James became Birmingham Mayor in 1853.

James Baldwin & Sons mainly produced square-bottomed bags, brown and white grocery bags and gun wadding, and by 1888 they had built a successful business with a large staff of skilled workers. The family carried on in business until 1984 when, then known as Baldwin (Cartons) Ltd, the company went into receivership. They had sold the Sherborne Mill in 1926 to King's Norton Paper Mill Ltd but had continued at the mill in Ladywood. The Sherborne Mill eventually became home to the Patrick Collection Motor Museum. The Ladywood Mill became a housing development.

IMPROVEMENTS IN BRASS

In 1830, a new method in brass manufacturing was developed. Mixing copper and zinc directly into the crucible proved quicker and more efficient than the previous cementation process. The cost was also reduced by using iron moulds instead of sand moulds because the iron ones could be reused and the finished article was of a better quality, so there was no need for filing to remove irregularities.

THE CHOCOLATE DYNASTY CONTINUES

In 1835, John Cadbury, the son of Richard Tapper Cadbury, rented a warehouse in Crooked Lane and from this warehouse a product was produced that is still a nation's favourite today.

John was born in Bull Street on 12 August 1801 and at the age of 15 he was sent to Leeds as an apprentice to a grocer. Like John's parents, the grocer was a member of the Society of Friends, so John made many acquaintances within the society. But were they a good influence?

John was very fond of music and had learnt to play the flute, but the study of music was considered an unacceptable pastime by the Friends due to its connections with frivolous activities, such as dancing. So, John gave up his music.

When he had completed his apprenticeship, his father sent him to London, where he worked in the tea industry for a year. Returning to Birmingham in 1824, he was encouraged by his father to set up a business as a tea and coffee dealer and with his father's help, he acquired premises at No. 93 Bull Street. However, shrewd investments meant he never had to ask for his father's financial help again.

The shop in Bull Street attracted many visitors, perhaps more so for the uniqueness of its frontage than the quality of the goods. His was among the first to introduce plate-glass windows in mahogany frames to a shop front. And he was particular in having his windows not only clean and bright but arranged in an attractive design.

But it was in the warehouse in Crooked Lane that his business ventures really took off and the Cadbury dynasty began. Here, he experimented, making cocoa and chocolate in a pestle and mortar. The rest is, of course, history.

In 1830, he began a career in public work, becoming involved in many committees. As well as taking a leading role in the search for a remedy for smoke pollution, he also campaigned against the use of young boys as chimney sweeps. At Hagley Hall, he showed, with the help of a scientific experiment, the ease with which a chimney could be cleaned by machine rather than young boys. To encourage a start in the reform, he bought a set of machines for himself. He also worked hard to broadcast the evils of alcohol and, like his father, became a total abstainer.

His first wife, Priscilla Ann Dymond, whom he had married in 1826, died after two years of marriage, but while visiting Lancaster a few years later, he met Candida Barrow. Falling madly in love, he married her in 1832. Unfortunately, this marriage did not last a lifetime either, as Candida was also to die in 1855, aged 49.

The warehouse was demolished by the Great Western Railway in 1847, at which time he moved to Bridge Street and his nephew, Richard Cadbury Barrow, took over the teashop. In 1861, John's sons George and Richard took over the business and then things really started to change for this well-known chocolate company.

A PRINCESS COMES TO TOWN

Birmingham, like the rest of the country, was entering a new age, the Victorian Age, as a new queen came to the throne. As a princess she had visited the factories of Birmingham with her mother, the Duchess of Kent, in August 1830. Among the factories she visited were Winfields, in Cambridge Street; Jennens & Bettridge, the papier-mâché manufacturers; and Edward Thomason's showrooms. And at Soho, she met William Murdoch and James Watt Jnr.

She stayed at Willdays Hotel in Temple Row and a company of infantry had waited near St Philip's Church as a guard of honour. When the royal party's arrival was imminent, the infantry moved down to the hotel to present arms as the royal carriage arrived. As Victoria stepped down, a lady named as Mrs Fairfax rushed to her and kissed her. Although the princess's mother and her attendants were angry, the crowd saw it as a harmless act of loyalty and cheered her.

BIRMINGHAM IN THE YOUNG QUEEN'S REIGN

With the Victorian Age came new techniques. Some industries benefited; some suffered.

One old established Birmingham trade found that with new technology, fewer workers were needed. In 1830 there had been 17,000 workers employed in the button industry and in the 1840s 600 million buttons were made. But by 1860, probably the same number of buttons, if not more, were made, but there were only 6,000 people working as button makers.

However, for the workers no longer being employed in the button industry there were many new industries being set up between 1830 and 1870 for them to try their hand at – including electroplating, chemicals, metal bedsteads, steel pens, plate glass and hydraulic machinery. And in 1870, it was said that the brass industry employed 10,000 workers.

However, conditions were not always good in the factories of Birmingham. In the early 1840s, children were working in the brass foundries where the air quality could be so polluted even adult workers might not live over the age of 45. Both boys and girls helped pump the bellows, but the boys also helped the casters. In the button industry, children as young as 6 were employed to help adult workers, and usually worked the same hours, often as long as twelve hours.

On the whole, these conditions only applied to the small and older factories and workshops. The newer or larger factories, such as Elkington, Winfields and Nettlefold & Chamberlain, gave their employees better working conditions.

Some wouldn't consider employing children under the age of 12, giving the jobs to women instead.

THE TRAIN NOW STANDING AT PLATFORM ONE

The first proposal for a railway line in Birmingham appeared in 1824. Shares in the Birmingham and London line were made available on 14 December and they proved very popular. Within two hours, 2,500 shares had been bought, but unfortunately for the shareholders the idea didn't take off and the project was abandoned.

Six years later, another idea was put forward and surveys were undertaken for the proposed positioning of the line and Broad Street was chosen as a possible site for the railway station. A Bill was put forward to the House of Commons on 20 February 1832, but it was rejected by the House of Lords.

A year later, fresh plans were drawn up and this time they were approved. Work began at the London end in July 1833 and at the Birmingham end in June 1834. Gradually, over the next four years sections were opened, until it was fully completed in August 1838. On 17 September, the first passenger train travelled the whole route.

While this was going on, other lines and stations were being built. The previous year, on 4 July 1837, a line had opened from Vauxhall Station to join the Manchester & Liverpool line near Warrington. In the first nine weeks, 7,374 passengers travelled to and from Manchester and a massive 18,666 travelled to and from Liverpool. The amount of money taken in ticket sales in those first two months added up to £41,943.

The departure of that first train from Birmingham caused a lot of excitement. Even at five in the morning people were gathering to witness the event. By six o'clock, every vantage point on the bridge across the line by the entrance of the station yard was taken. Then, at seven o'clock, a bell was rung and the train of eight carriages slowly emerged from the yard before picking up speed. As it made its way out of Birmingham, the train was greeted with cheers and the waving of hats and handkerchiefs from the spectators lining the route.

Other trains left during the day to similar admiration, but the crowds were also waiting for the first train to arrive from Liverpool. This train had left at 6.30 a.m., and was expected four and a half hours later, but due to all the crowds at various stops along the way, it arrived half an hour late at 11.30 to rapturous applause. With numerous other lines and stations opened around Birmingham and the rest of the country over the ensuing years, Birmingham was certainly now open for business.

A POPULAR DESSERT

Alfred Bird was born in Gloucestershire in 1811 and came to Birmingham to serve as an apprentice for a chemist in Digbeth. He opened his own shop in Bull Street. Of course, his name is now known all over the world and packaging with the name Bird on can be found in every supermarket. Bird's custard is loved by nearly everyone and it is all down to his wife.

Elizabeth Bird had an egg allergy, so her husband experimented and in 1837 came up with a recipe for an egg-free custard. Serving it to their dinner guests, he discovered how popular it was and decided to market it. The rest, as they say, is history.

The company remained a family business until 1947, when it was taken over by the General Food Corporation, but the name attached to Alfred's custard still lives on.

A well-loved dessert.

BILLY BUTTONS

On 3 May 1838, a character known as Billy Buttons died. Newspapers reporting his death said that no one had ever known his real name, but it was believed he belonged to a good family, as he became an officer in the navy when he was young. It was thought he was born around 1778.

Returning from a long voyage, the discovery that his sweetheart had died affected him badly and from then on, he began to lose his senses. Eventually, he became known for walking around the streets of Birmingham, constantly singing and collecting buttons, which he attached to his coat. When he died in a lodging house in Thomas Street, that coat weighed over 30lb.

ELECTRIFYING ORNAMENTS

George Elkington was born in Birmingham in 1801 and patented the first electroplating process for commercial use. By 1838, Elkington's was coating ornaments by dipping them in solutions of gold and silver at its factory in Newhall Street.

On 6 July 1838, the first patent was obtained for the electroplating process of covering copper and brass with zinc to produce tableware, jewellery and pens of a quality that were specifically aimed at high society. This was the invention of John Wright, a Birmingham surgeon. An article was placed in the liquid solution with a copper wire that carried an electric current. Electricity attacked the nitrate on silver and cyanide on gold, breaking up the chemicals, then distributing the gold and silver onto the surface. Those watching were often in awe that the surface of the bath was totally unaffected with no ripples showing on the surface.

In 1850, Elkington's employed 500 workers. Twenty years later, it was employing 1,000, and when George died in 1865 his son Frederick continued the family business. The Elkington factory has now become the Museum of Science and Industry.

A NINETEENTH-CENTURY ENTREPRENEUR

Josiah Mason arrived in Birmingham in 1816. He had been born in Mill Street, Kidderminster, in 1795, the son of a carpet weaver. At 8 years old, he was buying cakes and reselling them door to door. Later, he progressed to selling fruit and vegetables using a donkey to go from street to street. Other trades were experimented with such as baking, carpentry and carpet weaving before he decided to try his luck in Birmingham.

His uncle, Richard Griffiths, had a jewellery business so he went to work for him, then moved to pen manufacturing, working for a Mr Harrison in Lancaster Street. When he retired in 1824, Josiah bought the business for £500. Now aged 28, his flair for business and his inventive skills soon provided him with sucess. Building a machine for bevelling hoop-rings, he had made a profit of £1,000 in the first year.

In 1829, while walking down Bull Street, he passed Peart's bookshop. There, in the window, he spotted a card advertising nine pens for 3*s* 6*d*. He persuaded Peart to sell him one for 6*d*. Inspecting it closely, he knew he could make a better pen.

The pen he had bought was made by James Perry of London. So, once Josiah had perfected his pen, he sent some to them. Three days later, Perry turned up in Lancaster Street and offered Josiah a contract to make pens for him. In 1840, having become friends with George Elkington, he became a partner in the business and remained there until his retirement in 1856.

On 31 July 1869, he opened an orphanage in Erdington that housed 200 children. By 1889, this had increased to 350 children. It remained open until 1964, when the building was demolished. In 1872, he received a knighthood and on his 80th birthday, on 23 February 1875, he laid the foundation stone for a science college in Edmund Street. Known as the Mason Science College, it opened five years later, on his 85th birthday, and eventually became part of the University of Birmingham.

THE FIRST COUNCIL

On 31 October 1838, the Charter of Incorporation was introduced, and Birmingham was divided into thirteen wards. The first governing body of men were elected in December by the Burgesses and consisted of a mayor, that first one being William Schofield, plus sixteen aldermen and forty-eight councillors.

Nearly thirty years later, in 1862, councillors raised £200 to buy a mayor's chain of office. The first to wear it was Charles Sturge. Before 1879, the various departments of the Birmingham Corporation had been scattered around the town, but in 1879 the Council House was built.

THE PEOPLE OF BIRMINGHAM RIOT AGAIN

In 1837, with trade so bad, there was a feeling of unrest over the whole country. There had been a series of poor harvests and with the Corn Laws still being in operation, bread was very expensive. Wages were low and some factories were closing. Jobs were hard to find.

By 1838 there was nationwide unrest. The outcome was that a handful of MPs, after listening to the working classes, drew up the People's Charter, which outlined certain conditions to help them. The document was enthusiastically received and meetings to support it were held all over the country.

The first meeting in Birmingham was held on the evening of 13 August 1838 at Holloway Head. It was attended by an extremely large crowd.

These early meetings were peaceful but, after six months of not being heard, the leaders were suggesting more force was needed. On 1 July 1839, another meeting was planned in Birmingham, and prior to the meeting, groups began forming in the Bull Ring. To quell any possible riots, sixty men from the Metropolitan Force had been sent to the town and were positioned at the end of Moor Street while the mayor, William Schofield, seated on horseback, asked the demonstrators to disperse peacefully. When they ignored him, he signalled to the police to advance.

This antagonised the mob. They broke flag poles, which they used as weapons against the police, before being forced down Digbeth, up Bromsgrove Street and then to St Thomas' Church. Here, the mob equipped themselves with more weapons by ripping the railings from the walls. Eventually, by eleven o'clock that night, they had dispersed.

The Bull Ring, with the iron railings around Nelson's statue once again intact.

Two weeks later, on Monday, 15 July, another meeting was planned at Holloway Head and by two o'clock in the afternoon about 2,000 people had already arrived. Everything was quite peaceful at first, speeches were made, and afterwards it was suggested that an orderly march should be made through Birmingham. But it soon got out of hand as protesters charged down to the Bull Ring, and among the noise of voices was the sound of breaking glass as windows were shattered. Making their way to the Public Office in Moor Street, they tore more railings up in Bradford Street and Deritend High Street.

After smashing all the windows in the Public Office, they returned to the Bull Ring. Forcing the paving stones up, they threw them around and using railings from around Nelson's monument they battered down the doors and shutters of local shops. The contents from these shops were piled up outside and set alight. The local inhabitants were screaming for help, but the police were totally powerless among all this chaos.

Eventually the military arrived and the mob fled, leaving behind a scene of carnage and people complaining they had been left unprotected. Arrests were made and the sentences, depending on what proof could be found, alternated between transportation or imprisonment for one to eighteen months.

A CONSPIRATOR

One of those arrested was John Collins, the leader of the Birmingham branch of Chartists. He received a twelve month prison sentence. Born in Birmingham in 1802, into a working-class family, he was passionate about improving the lives of the working classes. As a member of the Birmingham Political Union he was one of their leading spokespersons.

While spending those twelve months in Warwick Gaol, he and fellow Chartist William Lovett, who had also been involved in the Birmingham riots, wrote the book *Chartism: A New Organisation of the People*. It showed how important it was for the working classes to have access to an education and the importance of entertainment other than drinking alcohol.

He travelled the country tirelessly giving lectures, but remained a Birmingham man and was elected a town councillor in 1847. He represented the district in which he lived – Ladywood. Sadly, he began to suffer from failing health in 1851 and died on 24 August 1852.

A POLICE FORCE FOR BIRMINGHAM

At the time of the riots, Birmingham had just thirty street-keepers and 180 nightwatchmen. On that day, 100 special constables had been sworn in, but the crowd had been too much for them. Something had to be done for this growing town, so an Act of Parliament was passed that gave Birmingham permission to set up its own police force.

Francis Burgess was appointed as the first Police Commissioner for Birmingham on 1 September 1839. A barrister practising from Warwick, he had also been in the 54th Foot Regiment and had been a captain at the Battle of Waterloo. He now had to recruit suitable men who were aged under 36 and 5ft 8in tall or more. They also had to be able to write and provide testimonials showing they had excellent character. Following interviews and medical examinations, 250 men were signed up on 30 November 1839. Their wage was 17*s* per week.

One of those first recruits was George Glossop. He went on to become the Chief Superintendent for Birmingham in 1860.

A NEW TYPE OF SHOP

In 1839, Birmingham had its first department store. It was a palatial building, standing at Nos 28 and 30 New Street, where two cottages had previously been, and known as Warwick House. Sometime in the early 1850s it was extended to include two neighbouring properties. Its owner, William Holliday, was a draper and now in this new-style shop, he could sell all types of fabrics and ribbons as well as ready-made clothes. There was also a carpet department.

FROM METAL TO GOVERNMENT

In January 1840, when Thomas Attwood resigned from Parliament, George Frederick Muntz won his vacant seat. He won by a majority of 539, around a 40 per cent margin. However, despite being a successful businessman, in politics he was very inconsistent. He would speak one way but vote another and friends found him eccentric and egotistical.

His father's family had now reinstated themselves in their French château (having previously lost it in the revolution), and his cousin George Louis Muntz was a member of the French Chamber of Deputies. It was thought that George wanted the same status for the English Muntzes.

At a political meeting at Bingley Hall, where he was giving a speech, George Dawson was also present. At the end, Dawson commented to a friend that newspapers wouldn't be able to print Muntz's speech as they wouldn't have enough I's.

In fact, George Muntz was most critical of anything published in the papers about him. So much so that he started his own newspaper – *The Birmingham Mercury*. He lost a lot of money through this newspaper and many of the debts weren't paid until after his death in 1857. But one claim to fame in his political life was that he was responsible for funding the introduction of perforated postage stamps.

THE REFORMIST

Joseph Sturge was born in Gloucestershire in 1793, the son of a farmer. At first, he tried his hand at farming but then moved to Bewdley in 1814 to work as a corn factor. He moved to Birmingham in 1822 and set up a corn dealership with his brother, Charles.

Nine years later, he left his brother in charge of the company while he concentrated on taking part in various campaigns for social reform. Having visited the Caribbean, he became particularly interested in the abolition of slavery and founded the British and Foreign Anti-Slavery Society in 1839.

He made three attempts to become an MP and although he was unsuccessful on every occasion, he did become involved in the movement for Parliamentary reform and the repeal of the Corn Laws.

He died in 1859, and his brother Charles went on to become Birmingham Mayor in 1862.

EVERYTHING TO EVERYBODY

Another advocate of social reform was George Dawson. He was born in London in 1821 and came to Birmingham in 1844 as the minister for the Mount Zion Baptist Church. But he left this church three years later and became the minister at the Church of the Saviour. His eloquence attracted a large following.

He was a great philosopher and developed the teaching of the 'civic gospel', which had a great influence on Joseph Chamberlain. The idea was that a town should be a community for everyone, and his sermons called for his congregation to join together to help reform the town, saying, 'The time has come to give everything to everybody.'

He was also an advocate for free education and although being a religious minister banned him from becoming a member of the council, he did join the Birmingham School

Board. His interest in English also promoted him to establish the Shakespeare Memorial Library in 1868 to allow everybody in Birmingham a chance to enjoy Shakespeare's works.

He died on 30 November 1876 and is buried in Key Hill Cemetery.

A BUSY DAY FOR A PRINCE

Prince Albert visited Birmingham regularly. His first visit was on 29 November 1843 when, while he and Victoria were visiting Sir Robert Peel at Drayton Manor, he took the opportunity to visit some of Birmingham's factories. Following that, he became very interested in the town and visited many other times.

On this first visit, he went to the glass works of Bacchus & Sons and watched the various ways used for blowing, heating, cutting and pressing. He then went to the rolling mills of Muntz and then to the papier-mâché works of Jennens & Bettridge. Here, after watching the various stages of manufacture, he visited the showroom, which held examples of tables, chairs, folding screens, cabinets and many other items. From there, he went to the gun and sword blade manufacturers, Messrs Sargant, where he was shown the process of rolling gun barrels, turning and boring them with the use of steam machinery. As he left the yard, workmen, some of whom had fought at Waterloo, fired the royal salute. He finished his tour of Birmingham with a visit to the Town Hall and the Free Grammar School.

But that first visit could have made him feel very different. He was accompanied by the mayor, Thomas Weston. Described as a wealthy man with loads of common sense, the mayor was not, however, used to the protocols of dealing with a person of royalty. After lunch, the prince and his equerry took their seats in the carriage, but Weston was nowhere to be found. They waited, and other dignitaries exchanged anxious looks as the prince was forced to put his overcoat on.

Eventually, the mayor came rushing out. He had lost his hat, and although there were others he could have borrowed, he had a large head and none of them fitted.

Luckily, Prince Albert saw the funny side of it and happily came to Birmingham again. This time he visited the exhibition at the Old Bingley Hall on 12 November 1849. The exhibition was entitled the Exposition of Art and Manufactures, and the prince enjoyed it so much it was often thought it had given him the idea for the Great Exhibition of 1851.

He visited again on 22 November 1855 and this time he laid the foundation stone for the Midland Institute.

KEEPING THE PEOPLE CLEAN

On 19 November 1844, a meeting was held to erect a public baths. A week later, £4,430 had been collected by subscriptions. A piece of land was eventually purchased in Kent Street in June 1846. After nearly five years, the baths were opened to the public on 21 May 1851 with attached washrooms available for the use of the working classes, although they weren't as popular as was hoped.

Other baths were opened in later years: one in Woodcock Street in August 1860, Northwood Street in March 1862, Sheepcote Street in 1878 and Ladywood in 1882.

PRESENTS FOR THE QUEEN AND HER CONSORT

On 28 May 1845, a deputation went to Buckingham Palace from the Jewellery Quarter to meet with Prince Albert. At the time, the manufacture of jewellery in Birmingham had become very depressed and the idea was to ask the prince to persuade his wife Queen Victoria to only wear British jewellery and therefore set an example. As gifts of persuasion, they presented Albert with a watch chain, seal and key for himself and an armlet, brooch, earrings and a waist buckle for the queen.

A WIRE FOR THE FUTURE

In 1847, James Horsfall patented a strong steel wire that he had secretly been experimenting with. He moved from Digbeth to Hay Mills, Yardley, and amalgamated with Webster's of Penn Mills, Sutton Coldfield. They supplied wire fine enough for the Redditch needle and fish-hook industry but strong enough for engines, machinery, colliery winding ropes and ships' rigging. They also supplied the French with the telegraph wire laid between Marseilles and Algiers. Then, when the original Atlantic wiring between England and America went dead, Webster & Horsfall's Patent Steel Wire was used to repair it. The work was completed in eleven months, which was ahead of schedule, and 1,600 tons of cable was used.

NOTHING STOPS A TRAIN

The 1840s brought many new railway lines, and the building of these brought about many negotiations with various people. One such person was a representative of the Society of Friends. The Great Western Railway (GWR) was going to slice through the Quakers' burial ground in Monmouth Street. This representative was said to be a well-known businessman, a Mr Broadbrim, and he was therefore insistent on a good deal that worked in his favour.

The railway directors found him a hard man to deal with. In the end, they were forced to hand over a large sum for what they considered a small amount of land. However, they had the last laugh in the end. After the contract was signed,

Mr Broadbrim discovered it didn't include the moving of the bodies buried in the ground. The GWR directors then asked for a large sum to arrange for the removal of the said bodies to the Friends Chapel in Bull Street.

A NEW STATION ON WHAT WAS ONCE A NEW STREET

The popularity of travelling by train soon made it a good idea for Birmingham to have a central railway station and the chosen place for this was New Street. So, in 1846, the clearing of the area began. Several streets were ripped up and £39,000 was paid to the Governors of the Grammar School to purchase land that belonged to them.

It took seven years to build the station and tunnels around it, but when finished its elaborate iron and glass roof, which stretched 1,080ft in length and sat 75ft high on its rails, was the largest in the world. The grand opening ceremony took place on 1 June 1853.

Inside New Street Station.

Once again, the railway had caused the disappearance of part of old Birmingham. With the building of the station, Lady Huntingdon's Chapel, King Street Theatre and Cannon Street Baptist Chapel disappeared.

In 1852, Snow Hill Station had been opened but its shed-like structure against this new wonderful station was much criticised, so it was rebuilt in 1871. More renovations took place between 1907–12 but by the 1960s many services were withdrawn in favour of New Street Station. It was then closed in 1972 and demolished. However, a new station was built in 1987.

BEFORE THE NEC

To make way for the north tunnel leaving New Street Station, Bingley House, once the home of the Lloyd family, had to be demolished. With a space left in the grounds, a temporary wooden hall was built to accommodate the Exhibition of the Manufactures of Birmingham and the Midland Counties in 1849.

The following year, it was decided to build a permanent hall. Bingley Hall was built with the cheap surplus of leftover steel columns from Euston Station, held together with red and blue bricks.

Holding between 20,000 and 25,000 people, for over 100 years it was home to cattle shows, dog shows, flower shows, motor shows, concerts and circuses. But disaster struck in January 1984. During a show for the Midland Caravan, Camping and Leisure Exhibition, the hall was damaged by fire. But with the National Exhibition Centre having been open for eight years it was felt there was no need to repair Bingley Hall and the building was demolished.

MAKING MORE MONEY

Ralph Heaton began his brass foundry in Slaney Street in 1794 before moving to the corner of Shadwell Street and Bath Street in 1808. His son, also Ralph, became an apprentice die-maker and once he had completed his training, he was given part of his father's factory to use as a workshop. Eventually, his own sons, Ralph and George, joined him. The company then became known as Heaton & Sons and was still in operation at the start of the twentieth century.

In 1850, Heaton purchased presses from an auction selling items from the Matthew Boulton estate and opened a mint in Icknield Street. Known as Heaton's Mint, it initially only made coins and tokens for the overseas market. But in 1853, he obtained a contract to produce coins for the Royal Mint. Ten years later, now known as the Birmingham Mint, he was employing 300 workers.

A PLACE TO STUDY

On 4 June 1852, a group of businessmen dined at Arthur Ryland's house and during the dinner the idea for the Midland Institute, a place for the working man to study, was born. Eventually, the idea was taken up by the council, and arrangements were made to raise money to purchase an appropriate piece of ground. Charles Dickens even visited and gave three readings at the Town Hall to help raise funds. Eventually, the foundation stone was laid by Prince Albert on 22 November 1855.

A CHRISTMAS CAROL

On 27 December 1853, Charles Dickens came to town to appear at an event held to raise funds for the Birmingham & Midland Institute. Regardless of bad weather, almost 2,000 people attended a reading given by Dickens at the Town Hall. He gave the crowd a lively and animated reading of his book, *A Christmas Carol*, which lasted three hours. Despite the lengthy performance, only a handful left before the end.

Two days later, he gave a reading of *The Cricket and the Hearth*, followed on 30 December by another reading of *A Christmas Carol*, for which Dickens insisted tickets should be mainly offered to the working class of the town. According to his opening speech, he did this in the hope that it would encourage them to use the facilities offered by the institute. These working classes showed their appreciation at the end of the reading with rapturous applause.

UNCLE TOM'S CABIN IN BIRMINGHAM

One of the most desirable locations on the Calthorpe estate was Wheeley's Hill, named after the family who had owned and farmed land there during the previous centuries. One particular piece of land was taken up by the newly arrived Joseph Sturge. Here he built No. 64 Wheeley's Road and lived there for thirty years.

As a campaigner for social reform, he also took an interest in what was going on in the USA. This prompted a secret visit from Harriet Beecher Stowe, author of *Uncle Tom's Cabin*, in 1853, while she was touring Britain. Longing for a few days' peace on her hectic tour, she accepted Joseph Sturge's invitation to his home. She and her party took the train from Edinburgh to Birmingham, where Joseph met them at the station. Harriet was soon sitting in Joseph's carriage on her way to Edgbaston with no one any wiser that she was in the vicinity. Her treat during the visit was having strawberries for breakfast.

A meeting was held at the Wheeley's Road house for other reformers. So many wanted to attend that the room was filled to capacity, and the windows had to be opened so that those who couldn't get into the house could listen from outside in the garden. Harriet was then taken back to the station to continue her journey to London.

In 1901, the house was bought by Barrow Cadbury. A tradition in the Cadbury family was that when they moved house, their previous house would be given to a charitable organisation. So, when Barrow and his wife eventually left in 1929, the house where the well-known female reformer had once stayed was given to the Young Women's Christian Association. It was turned into twelve small, bedsit-type flats.

INDUSTRY SPREADS TO THE SUBURBS

In 1853, W. Elliot & Sons, metal rollers and wire drawers, set up their factory up in Selly Oak, and remained there until the 1920s. Sturge's phosphorous factory also moved to Selly Oak. With two major businesses there, the small manor soon started to grow as houses were built for the workers to live near their places of work. Then Nettlefold & Chamberlain built a second screw factory in nearby Stirchley.

But smaller industries, which had started up in the suburbs, had still prevailed in these outer parishes, despite the new industries in Birmingham. Domestic workshops making nails were still in abundance in King's Norton, Northfield and Harborne.

A FUND RAISER

John Walsh was born in Mansfield, Nottinghamshire, but came to Birmingham to work for Pickford & Co. He left there to make soda water, then in 1851 he took over a glass factory in Hill Street that became so successful he moved it to Lodge Road. He was a member of the town council and worked hard to buy Aston Park for the town at a good price.

At the spring meeting in 1856, Walsh argued with other council members that they should buy the hall and park as it was so cheap. Another member, Ambrose Biggs, was at the other end of the room discussing the financial problems of the Queen's Hospital. The two conversations intertwined, and this gave Walsh the idea of having a fete at Aston to raise money for the hospital.

The fete was held on 28 July and hundreds of people came – not just locals, but people who had travelled on the train from the Black Country. Well-dressed people from Edgbaston mixed with pale-faced miners and tanned-faced agricultural labourers. There was music, dancing, merry-go-rounds, Punch & Judy shows, and a firework display in the evening.

A cheque was sent to the hospital for £1,500 and as the fete had been so successful, another was organised for 15 September. Following this, another cheque for £1,700 was handed over.

FAMILY HEIRLOOMS

Aston Hall has now become part of the Museums of Birmingham and family heirlooms can still be found in there. In the early 1700s, when the estate belonged to Charles Holte, his unmarried daughter, Mary, spent many hours working at her embroidery. In fact, she excelled at it. Today, two of her embroidered hangings are housed in Aston Hall. One is on display and shows the hall in stitched form, in all its splendour, together with red squirrels, the emblems of the Holte family. The other is too delicate to show and is kept in storage, but on this one Mary embroidered her name and age of 60. She remained a spinster her whole life.

A ROYAL VISITOR

On 15 June 1858, Queen Victoria visited Birmingham to open Aston Hall and Park. She also visited the Town Hall and knighted the mayor, Sir John Ratcliffe.

Long before the queen's arrival, the streets of Birmingham were crowded with flags, garlands and banners hanging everywhere. Platforms had been erected along the queen's route for people to gather and seats were erected for the Sunday schools to sit.

Arriving at the station at midday, the royal party passed through these decorated streets on its way to the Town Hall, where the Corporation delivered speeches of welcome. Then the mayor, an industrialist who had donated much to charitable organisations, received his knighthood. The royal carriages left the Town Hall at one o'clock and slowly drove through the crowds to Aston Hall amidst the peeling of church bells.

Lunch was served in one of the grand rooms of the hall for the royal party and afterwards, the queen went out on to a decorated balcony. After bands had played the National Anthem, she declared the house and gardens were now open to the public. She was given a tour of the house before leaving to spend the night at Stoneleigh Abbey.

PLAYING ON THE LAWN

In 1859, Major Thomas Henry Gem and his friend, Augurio Perera, a Spanish merchant, played a game of tennis on the lawns at Gem's home at No. 8 Ampton Court, Edgbaston. There doesn't seem anything unusual in this – except that tennis had never been played on grass before.

Since then, the women's 'warm-up' tournament before Wimbledon has been played at the Edgbaston Priory Club.

TRAGEDY IN THE GUN QUARTER

In 1859 working in the gun industry proved to be dangerous. On 27 September of that year, Pursall & Phillips, gun and ammunition manufacturers of Whittal Street, suffered a massive explosion and the whole factory went up in flames. Of the seventy workers in the building at the time, twenty were killed. Nineteen of them were women and girls with the age range of 10–31. One man, Humphrey Wood, died. He went back into the burning building to rescue his wife. Before he could get out, the factory had collapsed.

THE OLD TRADE CONTINUES

In Victoria's reign, as well as the more modern industries, Birmingham was still making leather goods. The Middlemore family had been making saddles since the early 1800s and by 1860 were employing 400 workers. Based at Holloway Head, they supplied saddles and accessories to the military and then, at the end of the nineteenth century, they began making bicycle saddles. For the manufacture of the bicycle saddles, they opened a new factory in Coventry. Then in 1920, they closed the Holloway Head premises and moved to Coventry.

AND THE GUN TRADE CONTINUES

The Birmingham Small Arms Company (BSA) was built on 25 acres of land in Small Heath in 1863. Since Richard Newdigate, groups of gun-makers had always pooled their resources together in times of war to help fulfil government contracts. So, on 7 June 1861, they formed a public company and the BSA went on to become the largest private arms manufacturer in Europe.

In times of peace, of course, there was a slump in production. In August 1878, the factory was forced to shut for twelve months and during this time the workers found employment digging and laying out the new Victoria Park in Small Heath. When the factory reopened in 1880, the directors were visited by an inventor who arrived riding an unusual bicycle, which was basically two wheels side by side, with the saddle between them. From then on, the BSA not only made guns, but bicycles as well and the Otto bike was born.

In 1903, a new idea presented itself to the BSA and soon a brand-new department was set up and the first motorcycle was produced in 1910.

BAUBLES AND SPARKLE

By the 1860s, most of Britain's jewellery came from Birmingham and varied from cheap to high-quality pieces. To escape the industrial growth in the centre of Birmingham, the small industrialists and merchants had moved into the Newhall estate during the late 1700s; in particular, the area around St Paul's and the then rural area of the Colmore estate. Brick terraced houses of two or three storeys tall were being built around what was then just a chapel. Each was large enough to contain a workshop so they were ideal for these smaller 'toymakers'.

Late in the 1830s, Elkington, Mason & Co. moved out to this new area, building large premises in Newhall Street. They were followed by penmakers Gillotts, who moved to Graham Street.

In the mid-nineteenth century, the gold rush in Australia introduced lower carats in gold alloys – 9, 12 and 15 carats. The fashion for jewellery now grew, with more people being able to afford it and in many instances, the 'toymakers' switched to making jewellery. The workshops spread along main streets, such as Warstone Lane, with the Vyse estate taking in more workshops.

The whole area now became known as the jewellery quarter. All the workers lived and worked there, with many of the workshops hidden away down alleyways. But different workers had different skills, and each contributed to the making of a certain piece, therefore they all needed to be close at hand to each other. The jewellery quarter became a close-knit community.

In the late nineteenth and early twentieth centuries, larger factories with better ventilation replaced some of the old buildings but there was still an abundance of family firms. In 1913, 70,000 people were employed in the jewellery trade in one form or another.

After the Second World War, the area enclosed by Vyse Street, Warstone Lane, Augustus Street and Northampton Street was demolished and the Hockley Centre was built. This eight-storey building opened in 1971.

A GUN WAS NO GOOD WITHOUT AMMUNITION

In 1863, George Kynoch established an ammunition factory. He had arrived in Birmingham from Scotland and started working as a bank clerk. He then went to work for Pursall & Phillips, a small arms factory in Whittall Street that made percussion caps. Following an explosion in 1859, which killed nineteen of its seventy workers, it was thought the factory should be moved to a more remote area.

George Kynoch became the owner of the factory and moved it out to a 4-acre site at Witton. Eventually, the factory, now known as G. Kynoch and Co., was spread out over 20 acres and employed several hundred workers. It used 50 tons of rolled brass, 100 tons of lead and 20 tons of gunpowder a week and, when necessary, was capable of producing 500,000 cartridges a day. They were soon making cartridges for the War Office.

In 1888, having become a Member of Parliament for Aston in 1886 and President of Aston Villa Football Club in 1887,

Kynoch resigned as a director of the company. But his luxury way of life brought him financial difficulties, so he sold his business, took out a partnership with Arthur Chamberlain and formed a new business – George Kynoch & Co.

Kynoch lived at Hamstead Hall, said to be one of the prettiest spots lying out on the outskirts. It was built on the summit of a hill surrounded by trees, so hiding the view of Hamstead Park Colliery. Here, Kynoch invited members of his constituency to sit and have picnics. Ramblers too, were encouraged to visit the fields and woods.

His wife, Helen, was well known for collecting, and she created what many people described as a museum. Theatrical items were a favourite of hers and she lovingly kept a scrapbook, in chronological order, of old posters from the Birmingham Theatre Royal. She was said to be the ideal hostess, and nothing was too much trouble when entertaining guests.

A BRIGHTER FUTURE

John Bright became an MP for Birmingham in 1858 and throughout the 1860s appeared at numerous protest meetings asking for reform in working and social life. One meeting, held at Brookfields in Birmingham, was attended by over 150,000 people.

His speeches were greatly admired, even by his opponents, and eventually, he and other Liberals brought Bills through Parliament that gave more people the right to vote, a better education system and better housing reforms. He remained MP for Birmingham until his death in 1889 – however, he was never a residen of the town.

VICTORIAN CHILDREN IN NEED

In 1862, Dr Thomas Heslop set up a hospital to care for sick children. He had been house physician at the General Hospital between 1848 and 1852, then lecturer and physician at Queen's Hospital and College.

His new hospital became known as the Birmingham and Midland Free Hospital For Sick Children. It first opened in an old mansion on Steelhouse Lane but then moved to Broad Street in 1870. Eventually, a purpose-built premises was provided for the Children's Hospital, which opened in 1917. However, since 1998 the hospital has been back on Steelhouse Lane, occupying the buildings previously used by the General Hospital.

THE WEIGHT OF POLITICS

Thomas Avery set up a firm manufacturing weighing scales with his brother, William. Known as W. & T. Avery Ltd, the business grew rapidly, but in 1864 Thomas left to become involved in politics. For the next thirty years, until his death in 1894, he was an alderman and helped develop the sewage and waterworks in Birmingham. In 1868 and 1881, he was Mayor of Birmingham.

LIBRARIES

A Public Library had been built in 1779 in Union Street with the help of John Lee, a button manufacturer. It went on to have 560 subscribers and housed 16,000 books. However, following a disagreement between these subscribers, some Anglican and some Nonconformists, as to the types of religious books the library should have, another library, large enough for 3,000 books, was built on Cannon Street.

In 1792, the Reverend Spencer Martin built a library next to the vicarage. Known as the Theological Library, it had been in existence since 1733, when the Reverend William Higgs had given it for the use of the clergy and religious students of the Birmingham district. He donated 550 books and bequeathed £200 for more books to be bought. When it closed in 1927, all the books were given to the Birmingham Library.

On 6 September 1865, the first lending library in Birmingham was opened. It was built on Edmund Street and became so popular it was extended. By the end of 1878, it contained 50,000 books, but unfortunately, on 11 January 1879, a fire broke out and 49,000 books were destroyed. The building was rebuilt and remained there until 1973, when it moved to new, larger premises at Chamberlain Square. The plans for this move had begun in 1938, but things were put on hold because of the Second World War. The library has since moved again, in 2013, to another new building in Centenary Square.

The old library in Ratcliffe Place.

A MAN OF INTEGRITY

Joseph Chamberlain, who was hardly ever seen without his eyeglass, was born in London but has always been adopted as being a Birmingham man. Born in 1836, he came to Birmingham in 1854 when his father joined the firm of Nettlefolds. Son followed father and advanced the firm. He was bright and perceptive and inspired confidence and admiration.

However, he was known for a certain amount of sarcasm in his speeches. On one occasion at a council dinner, he toasted the members who happily attended all the social events but didn't regularly attend the council meetings. It was his policy that if you took up a life in the public eye, you shouldn't be 'thin-skinned' and if someone 'gave blows', they should all be prepared to take them with a smile on their faces. On another occasion, George Dawson proposed his health and referred to his slender stature, saying he wished there was more of the mayor to look at. In reply, Chamberlain jokingly said, 'Mr Dawson has been good enough to refer to me as a Mayor without a Corporation.'

Joseph had strong republican ideals and was known to stay seated when the royal toast was made. However, when the Prince and Princess of Wales visited in 1874 his speech and actions didn't give him away. In his private life, people who had met him with trepidation found he wasn't the ogre they had expected. In fact, away from his public life he was quite quiet and inoffensive.

When he was elected a Member of Parliament in 1876, his municipal career ended, but this new career proved successful too. Within a few years he had become a Cabinet minister and is well known for his Act of Parliament for the Welsh water project.

His first wife died giving birth to their son, Austen, in 1863. Joseph then married her cousin, Florence, in 1868 and their son, Neville, who followed his father into great things, was born in 1869. Florence also died in childbirth in 1875.

In 1863, Joseph lived at Moor Green Hall near Moseley, then in the 1880s, Highbury – named after the district in London where Joseph was born – was built.

FAMILY DYNASTY

The Chamberlain family were very active in Birmingham municipal life. Joseph's brother, Richard, was mayor in 1879 and 1880. He was very public spirited and popular but unfortunately died young in 1899.

Another brother, Arthur, was also a town councillor, although he didn't stay long and became a local magistrate.

Joseph's sister married William Kendrick, who was MP for the Northern Division of Birmingham and had also been mayor in 1877. He did much for education and philanthropic causes.

Joseph's son, Austen was MP for a Worcestershire Division and had also won the Nobel Peace Prize. And of course, there was his other son, Neville – but he will be spoken about later.

FACELIFT

When Joseph Chamberlain was elected a member of the Birmingham Town Council in 1869, he was full of ideas, and he persuaded friends to also become candidates in order to gain support. In his younger days, Chamberlain would walk from his lodgings in Edgbaston to his Broad Street office, so he saw first-hand some of the slum areas. He talked to the people living in them and knew something would need to be done. Unfortunately, his ideas put Birmingham into debt. In 1869, the debt amounted to £588,000 and within ten years it had risen to £6,212,000.

But with all the changes, Birmingham was prospering, thanks to Chamberlain. He had improved sanitation; the streets and lighting had improved; and the general ambiance was better. Trees had been planted along some of the main thoroughfares, although at first they had struggled and had to be replanted.

On becoming mayor in 1873, he had decided to buy the gas and water supplies and although the shareholders weren't happy, they did receive a return of £1.9 million for gas and £1.35 million for water. But it was the Artisans' Dwelling Act in 1875 that gave Chamberlain his chance to really make a difference. The act allowed him to buy up slum areas and demolish houses and streets. His plan was to make a new main street through Birmingham.

However, there was a problem. The lease stipulated that if a new building was meant for shops or offices it could be many storeys high. This meant that any smaller buildings were robbed of light. The people in these properties demanded compensation, only to find they were not covered by the Act. The other problem was that some were established businesses and were identified by their premises – but they were forced to move. The result was that rather than move to another building, the shopkeeper just retired or discontinued his business. Even shopkeepers who didn't work in this new area were affected. When the new street was built, it took traffic away from certain streets that had once been busy thoroughfares. Soon shops on these streets became less busy.

Victorian shopping in Birmingham.

Despite all these problems, once finished, it was noticeable that the new shops were of a much better class and attracted more shoppers. Previously, Birmingham had been looked down on, with many people shopping elsewhere. They went to Leamington Spa, Cheltenham or even London. But after Corporation Street was completed, people flocked to Birmingham, where department stores were appearing and they could get everything under one roof.

THE FIRST SHOPPING CENTRES

With Birmingham becoming a place to go, places where shoppers could shop in comfort and undercover were needed. Shopping arcades were already popular with the middle classes in London, so now Birmingham felt the need to follow suit.

The Great Western Arcade.

The first was built between Monmouth Street and Temple Row and opened on 26 August 1876. It contained thirty-eight shops and fifty-six offices in the balconies above. The Central Arcade, which joined Cannon Street and Corporation Street, opened on 26 September 1881 and included a large restaurant.

On 5 April 1884, a continuation of the Temple Row arcade opened. Known as the Great Western Arcade, it now extended to Colmore Row and added another twenty-six shops.

The Imperial Arcade in Dale End, with thirty-two shops and offices, opened in time for Christmas 1883. Snow Hill Station had its own arcade and the Hen & Chickens Hotel had one attached to the hotel.

THE ROUNDHOUSE

In 1874, a unique building was built on Sheepcote Street, close to both the canal and the railway. A large, red-bricked, circular building, it was used as a stables and stores for the Birmingham Corporation Public Works Department. It was also a base for the lamp lighters. A competition had been held by the Corporation to find a design for the building and this was won by William H. Ward.

Over the years, the building has been used for many things and had periods of dereliction, but it has now undergone huge renovation, thanks to the National Trust and the Canals & River Trust, and is now open to the public.

Ward was responsible for many other buildings in Birmingham, including hotels, some of the buildings in Corporation Street, the Workhouse and the Great Western Arcade.

THE BEAUTIFUL GAME

In 1858, 31 acres of the Aston estate – which had been the kitchen garden – had become known as the People's Park and was run by the Birmingham Corporation. In 1874, a group of young men from the Villa Cross Wesleyan Chapel formed a football team, calling themselves the Aston Villa Wesleyan Chapel. They were to become known as just Aston Villa. Taking over the lease of the People's Park in 1892, they developed the Aston Villa football ground over a period of five years.

The Small Heath Alliance Football Club was formed in 1875, and they went on to become known as Birmingham City. They first played at a ground in Muntz Street, but by 1906, the ground had become too small for the club. A new pitch was constructed in Bordesley and became known as St Andrew's.

When they first formed, visiting teams arrived on a Saturday for matches from as far afield as Sheffield, but it was not until the 1890s that football became a spectator sport and then, separated by just over 2 miles, the rivalry between the two teams became, and still is, quite fierce.

A NEW COMMUNITY WITH A FRENCH NAME

In 1878, building work commenced on just over 14 acres of land by a small river named the Bourne near Selly Oak. With the canal and railway line running alongside it, it was an ideal spot, and over the ensuing years a factory, together with its model village, began to take shape.

John Cadbury had originally opened his grocery store next to his brother, Richard Tapper Cadbury, in Bull Street in 1824, but when his sons, George and Richard Cadbury, took over the business in 1861, it had already become a chocolate shop.

George saw how his workers lived in the increasing squalor of back-to-back courtyard housing. He had watched with interest how Joseph Chamberlain had cleared some of these buildings and improved living conditions, so he decided to do the same. He would move the entire factory, together with his workers, out of the city and into the countryside.

The new development was given the French-sounding name of Bournville because at the time, French chocolate was the best on the market. But soon, Cadbury chocolate was earning its reputation still known today. Its famous bar, Dairy Milk, appeared in 1905 and soon became a firm favourite. By 1925, it was then the UK's bestselling chocolate bar. But it might not have been known as Dairy Milk. Two other names were suggested at the time – Dairy Maid and Highland Milk.

In the early days, probably well into the twentieth century, the Cadbury family didn't believe in married women working and therefore only employed unmarried girls. When the day came for a young girl to end her employment prior to her wedding day, she would be summoned to George's office. There she would be given a Bible and a carnation. The carnation was George's idea. He loved flowers and took a bunch every day, from either the garden or his greenhouses, to his office to hand out to any visitors. The giving of a Bible dates back to when the business was still on Bridge Street.

George Cadbury himself lived at No. 32 George Street, Edgbaston, before buying 'Woodbrooke' on the Bristol Road from Frederick Elkington in 1881. The large house is now a college for research and teaching in Quakerism.

In 2010, the business was taken over by Kraft for £11.5 billion with a promise that the Cadbury name and reputation would remain.

In 2024, to celebrate their 200th anniversary, Cadbury produced replicas of their early wrappers such as this one from 1940.

THE HEIRESS

The first public park in Birmingham had been opened in 1857 by the Duke of Cambridge, on land that Lord Calthorpe had donated on the Pershore Road and Balsall Heath Road. In 1875, Louisa Ann Ryland gave 250 acres of land to Birmingham for the construction of a park. This park is now Cannon Hill Park – Louisa had refused the suggestion it should be called Ryland Park.

Louisa was born in 1814 at 'The Laurels' in Edgbaston, the only child of Samuel Ryland and his wife, Anne Pemberton. Her mother died when she was only a baby and she and her father moved to 'The Priory' in Warwick. Then, when the Great Western Railway was cut through their grounds, they moved to their estate in Sherbourne.

By now Louisa was growing up and her father wanted to find a good marriage for her. He even considered Lord Brook of Warwick. But Louisa was in love with a Henry Smith, who her father didn't consider good enough. With obstacles put in their way, Henry gave up his quest for Louisa's hand and married Maria Phipson. He went on to become Mayor of Birmingham in 1851.

Louisa never married but lived at Barford Hall with her companion, Charlotte Randell. Samuel died when she was only 29 and she was left a wealthy young lady with estates scattered around Ladywood, Sparkhill, Small Heath, Northfield and Moseley.

Despite her family having left Birmingham, she never forgot her roots and most of her money went to the town. After her gift of land for Cannon Hill Park in 1879, she gave land for Victoria Park in Small Heath, together with £4,000 towards the cost of developing it. Further donations included £25,000 for the General Hospital, £10,000 to the Midland Institute and £10,000 towards the salaries of the teachers at the School of Art.

She died in 1889, and faithful to the man she had loved, the main beneficiary of her will was Henry Smith's son, Charles. The only condition was that he took the name Ryland. The descendants of Charles Alston Smith-Ryland still own land in Barford and Sherborne today.

A SAD END

John Skirrow Wright was born in London, but the family moved to Birmingham in 1824, and by 1834, his father was a manager at the Birmingham, Stourbridge & Wolverhampton Canal Company. In 1838, John found himself a job as a junior clerk at the button factory of Smith & Kemp in Brearley Street. He showed good potential and was quickly promoted through the ranks, and in 1850 he became a partner. When Kemp retired in 1858, the company became known as Smith & Wright, then when Smith died in 1876 John Wright became the sole partner.

A career in politics saw him being based in Nottingham, but he remained living in Birmingham, at Mentone House, Church Hill, Handsworth. His big achievement was that he introduced the postal order, which allowed anyone who did not have a bank account to be able to use something similar to a cheque.

On 15 April 1880, he was attending a meeting at the Council House when it was noticed he had fallen asleep and was snoring loudly. When he couldn't be roused, it was realised he wasn't just asleep, he had suffered a seizure. By the time the doctor had arrived he was dead.

A SCIENTIFIC LADY

Constance Naden was born at No. 15 Francis Road, Edgbaston, on 24 January 1858. Sadly, two weeks after her birth her mother Caroline died, so she was sent to live with her grandparents, Caroline and Josiah Woodhill at Pakenham House, Edgbaston. When she was 8 years old, she attended the local Unitarian school, and it was here she discovered a joy for painting. One of her paintings, 'Bird's Nest and Wild Roses', appeared at the Spring Exhibition of the Birmingham Society for Artists in 1878.

Constance went on to study botany and French at the Birmingham and Midland Institute in 1879, then later– between 1881 and 1887– she studied science, geology and zoology at the Mason Science College. By now, she had made friends with Robert Lewins MD, and together they developed hylo-idealism, a philosophy that we are the makers of our own cosmos and our perceptions are merely subjective ideals.

But it is as a writer of poems and essays that she is most known and for which she won several awards. Her first book of poems, *Songs and Sonnets of Springtime*, was published in 1881.

When her grandmother died in 1887 she was left a large inheritance. With this she spent the next twelve months travelling across the Middle East and Asia with her friend, Madeline Daniell, a women's activist. She became extremely interested in India, so when she returned to England she set up a fund to enable Indian woman to study medicine.

But her life was tragically cut short when she was diagnosed with having infected ovarian cysts. Although an initial operation was successful, she died two weeks later on 23 December 1889, aged 31. She was buried in Key Hill Cemetery, where her gravestone describes her as 'Poet, Scientist and Philosopher'.

A BOOK FIFTEEN YEARS IN THE WRITING

Joseph Henry Shorthouse was born on Great Charles Street in 1834. His family had settled in Birmingham in the eighteenth century and set up as pharmacists in Newmarket Street. On completing his education, Joseph joined the family business. However, that is not what he became famous for.

As a boy he had enjoyed writing and continued this as a young man by joining a writers' club that met in Birmingham during the winter. He remained a member of this group for twenty-five years. For years, he had an idea in his head for a novel, but it wasn't until 1865 that he began to commit pen to paper. He then spent another ten years writing it, often leaving it untouched for weeks, months, even years at a time. Even after he had finished the book, it was just left on one side. When asked why, he said he didn't think a publisher would be interested in it so he wasn't going to bother to try. Eventually, he was persuaded to get some copies printed and in July 1880, 100 copies were handed out to friends.

Set in the seventeenth century, it was called *John Inglesant* and told a romantic story of the intrigues between the Church of England, the Catholic faith and one man's fight to decide who he is. Joseph himself had left his faith of Quakerism behind to convert to the Church of England in 1861.

One of his friends passed their copy to the niece of a well-known literary critic, Matthew Arnold. Mrs Humphrey Ward showed it to the publisher Macmillan and they immediately wanted to publish it. When Prime Minister Gladstone read it and publicised the fact that he had thoroughly enjoyed it, sales soared. In no time at all, 30,000 copies had been sold. The book, which Joseph had said people wouldn't like, found itself on bookshelves in America and on the Continent and its author found himself having breakfast at No. 10 Downing Street.

Joseph went on to write other novels, but none were as successful as his first. He died in Edgbaston in 1903 and is buried in the churchyard there.

WAS SHERLOCK A BRUMMIE?

Here is another writer, not from Birmingham, but the fact he spent a few years in town does mean that he deserves a mention here.

Arthur Conan Doyle lived at Clifton House, Aston, between 1878 and 1881 and worked as a chemist and assistant to Dr Reginald Ratcliffe-Hoare, who has supposedly been immortalised as Dr Horton in *The Stark Munro Letters*. Conan Doyle's first story, *The Mystery of Sasassa Valley*, was written in Birmingham in 1879. But did one of his later novels, *The Hound of the Baskervilles*, perhaps take inspiration from the name of a famous Brummie?

SCREWS, NUTS AND BOLTS

John Nettlefold began making screws in 1834 after moving to Birmingham from London. He'd seen how successful Birmingham was becoming, so he wanted to be part of it. He set up Nettlefold & Son Ltd in Baskerville Place, and twenty years later he passed the reins over to his son, Joseph, and his nephew, Joseph Chamberlain.

With this new partnership, the firm became known as Nettlefold & Chamberlain and by 1865 was employing 2,000 workers. Eventually, with Chamberlain's political success, his cousin took sole control of the business, and the company name changed to Nettlefold & Co. When Joseph Nettlefold died in 1881, his younger brother, Frederick, took over and the firm became known as Nettlefolds Ltd.

Meanwhile in 1856, Arthur Keen, the son of a farmer, was setting up business as a nut and bolt manufacturer. Impressed by Nettlefolds, he used them as a model for his business ambitions, although he wasn't initially as successful. But in 1899, he bought the Dowlais Iron Company from Ivor Guest in Wales and then in 1902 merged with Nettlefolds.

And so, GKN, using the names Guest, Keen and Nettlefold, was born and is now a well-known worldwide company.

BEER AT HOME

Charles Kirkham was a maker of sarsaparilla beer and lived at Hamstead Hall between 1881 and 1884. He seems to have been quite a character and was conspicuous by the heavy fur-lined coat he wore, even when it wasn't that cold, and the pony he rode covered in small bells to attract everyone's attention.

During his time at Hamstead Hall, he opened the grounds and visitors were entertained by gymnasts and clowns. Two unique attractions were a huge whale, carried on carts joined together to make a large platform, and a lady whose hair was so long she plaited it and attached it to a small cart, which she dragged along behind her.

NOT AN ORIGINAL BIRMINGHAM BUSINESS

In 1655, Thomas Firmin set up his business, Firmin & Sons. Born in Suffolk in 1632, he moved to London and became an apprentice to a belt-maker. Setting up on his own, his first premises were in Lombard Street. Then in 1882, a factory was opened in Birmingham, which has now become the headquarters of the company, based in New Town Row.

They are the oldest manufacturing company in England, which supplies the military with buttons, badges and parade dress and received a royal warrant in 1796. Still making ceremonial accessories and dress for the Household Cavalry and Artillery Company, they still have the button dies that were used to strike buttons for uniforms in the Napoleonic Wars and for Lord Nelson's uniform.

NO WINE IN THE BAR

In August 1883, the Birmingham Coffee House Company opened the Cobden Hotel, which had cost £30,000 to build. It had been named after Richard Cobden, who had been an activist for reform in the 1840s and a colleague of John Bright. A strong supporter of the temperance movement, the coffee house had opened as an alternative to drinking liquor and for this reason the hotel was unlicensed.

A corner hotel, it sat at the junction of Corporation Street and Cherry Street with its Gothic doorway entrance on Cherry Street. In the basement were three elegantly fitted rooms – a coffee room, smoke room and luncheon room – which, being in the basement, were well lit with artificial lighting. The walls were decorated with tiles of various styles and the bar, on the ground floor, matched with the same decoration. There was also a billiard room. The building contained 130 bedrooms with the laundry and kitchens on the top floor. There were around ninety members of staff to cater for the wishes of the hotel's guests. The public opening was attended by John Bright.

A new building was bought in 1959 on the Hagley Road and the hotel is still in operation there today. Of course, it is no longer a temperance hotel. The site at Cherry Street was taken over by Rackham's department store.

THE SPORT OF KINGS

The Sutton Park Racecourse had existed in the Longmoor Valley since the 1830s but the clerk of the course decided it needed improvements. So, it closed down on 20 August 1879.

John Sheldon then set about producing an updated course. He bought 250 acres of ground at Four Oaks Park for £60,000 and began laying out a circular track around Four Oaks Hall, which would provide both flat racing and national hunt racing. He built what were described as 'spectacular' grandstands, which held 5,000 people. The first meetings were held on 17 and 18 March 1881 and crowds of racegoers walked to the racecourse from Four Oaks Railway Station.

The racecourse wasn't a success, and making no profit, it was sold in August 1890. The land was bought by Lord Clanricarde and it became part of the Four Oaks private estate.

Later, two brothers, John and Stanley Ford, opened the Bromford Bridge Racecourse and the first meetings here were held on 14 and 15 June 1895. The Midland Welter Handicap was run over a mile and a quarter.

When the suffragettes burnt down the grandstand in 1914, the course was bought by the military as a site for barrage balloons and other anti-aircraft measures. After the Second World War the Birmingham Racecourse Company bought it for £85,000 and it reopened in 1946.

Low attendances in the 1960s saw the final meeting on 21 June 1965. It was sold for £1.25 million to the Birmingham Corporation, which used it for a new housing development with all the roads given horse racing names – Newmarket Way, Haydock Close, Thirsk Croft.

THE GOLDEN BOOT

Howard Vaughton, the grandson of Philip Vaughton of the jewellery company, was born in 1861 and didn't follow in the family business at first. Instead, he became a footballer. He played for Aston Villa, joining them in the 1880–81 season, and then was part of the team that won the FA Cup in 1887. He also played for his country. The first time was in February 1882, and he is still high on the list of top scorers in international matches, although his shooting was described by other players as being erratic.

But he didn't just play football. He also won the All-England Skating Championship, played both cricket and hockey at county level, raced in cycling events and was an excellent swimmer.

In May 1888, he suffered a thigh injury and was forced to retire from football and return to the family business. However, in June 1924 he was appointed President of Aston Villa and then became a director, a post he remained in until 1932. He died in January 1937.

LEATHER ON WILLOW

The town's first cricket club, the Birmingham Cricket Club, had been formed in 1819 for members of the young 'elite'. The pitch was in a field in Ladywood. However, it was on 8 April 1882 that, at a meeting in Leamington Spa, the Warwickshire County Cricket Club was formed.

With a permanent home needed for the club, it was suggested that somewhere in either Rugby or Leamington Spa would be suitable, but as Birmingham had a larger population, a 12-acre field on the Calthorpe estate was chosen. Four years later in June 1882, the first matches were played. A crowd of 3,000 attended. Two months later, the Australian team played and 6,000 attended.

In 1902 the first test match was played at the ground, again against the Australians, and a permanent stand was built for the occasion. In 1911, Warwickshire won its first county championship title, and since then Edgbaston Cricket Ground has become one of the top grounds in cricket circles.

In 1932, with various county boundaries having been changed over the years, the county boundary for the cricket counties of Warwickshire and Worcestershire was the River Rea and not the local government boundary. During a match with the Indian team, C.K. Nayudu hit a ball bowled by Jarrett over the River Rea and 80 yards across the playing field on the other side – and therefore into Worcestershire territory.

A HANGING TOWN

Birmingham had become an assize town in 1859, but it wasn't until July 1884 that the first assizes took place. So now, Winson Green Prison, which had been built between 1845 and 1849, became a hanging prison and the first hanging that took place there was for Henry Kimberley.

Emily Palmer was a friend of Henry Kimberley's common-law wife, Harriet Steward, who had recently separated from Henry. He had followed both Emily and Harriet from the Gem Spirit Vault in Steelhouse Lane, where Emily's husband was the landlord, to the White Hart in Paradise Street. Here he threatened Harriet that if she didn't go back to him he would shoot her. Emily tried to intervene, but Henry drew a gun, shot Harriet and then Emily. Harriet survived but Emily died two weeks later.

Henry's execution took place on 17 March 1885 and about 15,000 people stood outside Winson Green Prison, waiting to see the black flag raised to denote that it had taken place.

THE NEW COURTHOUSE

On 23 March 1887, the foundation stone was laid for the new Victoria Law Courts, and it was Queen Victoria herself who performed the ceremony.

Arriving at Small Heath station at 1 p.m., she was escorted by soldiers, policemen and firemen through the crowded streets to the Town Hall. After a fanfare of trumpets and a short musical presentation, she attended a small private lunch. Afterwards, a procession left for Corporation Street, where the stone was laid out ready for her. She gave it three taps with an ivory mallet, then left for Snow Hill Station.

The Victoria Law Courts were officially opened in 1891 by the Prince and Princess of Wales. Built of red brick and terracotta, the building was designed by Sir Aston and Ingress Bell, who had won the contract through an open competition.

THE BIRTH OF THE FOOTBALL LEAGUE

In 1888, William McGregor moved to Birmingham from Perthshire. He became involved with Aston Villa under various roles – namely president, director and chairman.

In those days, football matches were often cancelled for various reasons so, in 1888, he suggested an idea to other clubs in England that culminated in the Football League being born. This now meant that there was a regular fixture list and football moved from being a game played by amateur players looking for a hobby to being a profession.

A CITY IS BORN

The growth of Birmingham in the 1800s had proceeded at an alarming rate. At the start of the century the population was 78,760, living in 16,659 homes. When the first census was taken in 1841, the population had risen to 182,922, with properties of some description amounting to 36,238. By the end of the century, it was 522,204. This huge increase surely made it more of a city than a town?

On 14 January 1889, Birmingham did indeed become a city. But it was a city without a cathedral. It was sixteen years later that St Philip's became a cathedral and the Diocese of Birmingham was formed.

It was on 31 October 1838 that Birmingham had been given its Charter of Incorporation, so when the fiftieth anniversary was approaching and the town was growing rapidly, it was thought a good idea to approach the Home Secretary to ask if it was possible for Birmingham to be given city status. The queen gave her permission and the town, which people from abroad had already been calling a city because of its size, became a city.

WHO WERE THE REAL PEAKY BLINDERS?

There have been many suggestions as to how the Peaky Blinders got their name, but during the late 1880s and early 1900s, they were a gang who terrorised Birmingham and who seem to have originally emerged from the Small Heath area. They were not afraid of violence and certainly didn't appear to be afraid of the police.

One such case in July 1897 saw Police Constable George Snipe die from injuries received while police were trying to control a street fight on Bridge Street West. A brick had been thrown by George 'Cloggy' Williams, whose hair was described in newspapers as being short at the back and pulled down in a fringe over his forehead, which was said to be the approved Peaky Blinder style.

There were rival gangs of Peaky Blinders, who also referred to themselves as 'sloggers', and this usually caused a great deal of problems for the police. In December 1893, John Metcalf was found lying on the ground in crowded Digbeth, bleeding to death and yet, apart from a scuffle, no one had heard anything. He belonged to the Park Street Gang and one of their members had had an argument with a member of the Barford Street Gang. Metcalf had gone in search of him and got more than he bargained for.

Of course, the police found it difficult to find the culprit at first, as no one apparently saw anything. But eventually, they arrested John Cherry. After he'd been found guilty of manslaughter, the judge appeared lenient as he said the attack was just done in the heat of the moment and Cherry may not have realised that the cut he gave Metcalf would cause his death. He sentenced him to five years.

In a way that was typical of what we know of the Peaky Blinders, who cared nothing for authority. John Cherry's reaction was to smile, look up at the gallery and laugh, then skip gaily out of the dock.

A QUAINT STREET NAME

During the 1800s a footpath led from Holloway Head to Edgbaston Church. It became known as Speaking Stile Lane because, from a stile on this short lane, there was an exceptional echo. It did eventually become a small residential area in the late 1800s that retained the name.

FROM CABINETS TO COFFINS

The Newman Brothers Coffin Furniture Works was opened in 1894 on Fleet Street and was also known as the Fleet Works. Alfred and Edwin had worked in the brass industry since 1882, making cabinet fittings, but they noticed what big business funerals had become. Realising the handle on a cabinet was the same as a handle on a coffin, they went into the coffin accessory business, making anything from handles to name plates.

However, although the Newman Coffin Furniture Works remained in business until 1998, the brothers' partnership didn't last. A year after establishing the business, Edwin was being taken to the bankruptcy courts. Later, he seems to have gone back to just making cabinet handles again. The business was taken over by Alfred's sons in 1933.

Through the years Newman Brothers made the accessories for the coffins of many well-known names in both the political world and the royal family, including Joseph Chamberlain, Winston Churchill, George V and VI, the Queen Mother and Princess Diana.

AN URGENT ORDER

On 5 September 1895, someone calling himself 'Mr Jones' visited the Birmingham Small Arms Factory in Armoury Road, Small Heath. He introduced himself as the assistant secretary of the British South Africa Company and said he wanted to purchase as many Lee Melford rifles as was possible. More importantly, they needed to be on a ship leaving Southampton for Cape Town the following night.

By nine o'clock the following morning, 2,000 rifles had been prepard and 1 million cartridges had been found and packed. A special train rushed them to Southampton, where they were loaded on to the SS *Scott* bound for South Africa.

Three months later, on 29 December, the Jameson Raid took place, which saw the lead-up to the Boer War. Rumour tells that these Birmingham guns were used in that assault.

THE VALLEY OF CHILDHOOD

Anthony Bunn Johnson originally set up his toy factory around 1820, but in 1860, his sons, Joseph and Alfred, set up Johnson Brothers, stationers, printers and bookbinders in George Street, Harborne. Then, in 1897, Joseph and his son, Alfred J., moved the business to new premises at Rose Road in Chad Valley, situated between Harborne and Edgbaston, which took its name from the small Chad Brook that ran from Harborne to the River Rea. After their move, they began specialising in producing children's toys and board games, which in 1915 included a high-quality teddy bear.

In 1919 the factory was extended and changed its name to Chad Valley Toys. During the Second World War they also produced parts for anti-aircraft guns as well as providing jigsaws, chess sets and dominoes for the armed forces and hospitals. Through the 1950s and '60s, they invested in other toy companies but by the early 1970s had run into financial difficulties. They sold the business to Palitoy and the Harborne factory was demolished in 1973. But the Chad Valley trademark survived. In 1988, it was bought by Woolworth's and when that firm closed it was taken on by Argos.

A NIGHT AT THE CIRCUS

In 1899, the circus came to town in the form of Wombwell's Menagerie and the town was enthralled by the collection of exotic animals. However, before the performance on 27 September, one of the lions escaped and, slipping through a flap in the circus tent, it went on a tour of the streets of Aston.

It managed to get down an opening into the sewers and could be heard roaring through every manhole as it wandered about the underground network. Eventually, the ringmaster, Frank Bostock, settled the crowd, blew a horn and lifted a cloth that was covering a cage – lo and behold, there was the escaped lion. Or was it?

Everyone went home happy having enjoyed a night at the circus, unaware that the lion they had seen in the cage was a second one and the one that had escaped was still down in the sewers. The following day, Bostock admitted the deception to the police, who gave him an option – send his men down to find it and capture it or they would go down and shoot it.

Bostock sent two members of staff down into the sewers. Banging the pipes with a shoe, shouting and waving a lantern, they managed to encourage the beast to an opening where a trap had been placed. Tying its hind legs with rope, Bostock dragged it back up to the surface.

With all the commotion, people had gathered to see what was happening. As soon as they saw the lion there was complete panic. People were climbing lampposts; some were running in all directions and others were banging on doors asking to be let in.

The entourage left town the following morning, but it was a long time before the people of Aston forgot their night at the circus.

OLD JOE ARRIVES

On 31 January 1898, Joseph Chamberlain proposed the idea of uniting the Mason College and the Queen's College to form the University of Birmingham. By February 1899, £326,500 had been raised and Birmingham University was established on 1 October 1900.

Then Lord Calthorpe gave 25 acres of ground at Bournbrook for a new building to be erected. Designed by Sir Aston Webb, it was completed in 1909 and officially opened by Edward VII on 7 July 1909. Standing tall over the university is the Joseph

Chamberlain Memorial Clock Tower. At a height of 100ft, it is quite a spectacle in the area and is affectionately known as 'Old Joe'.

For a time, the medical school remained at the Queen's Hospital and General Hospital but when the need for a new hospital arose, the Cadbury brothers offered land adjacent to the university for the building of a new hospital, and therefore a place near the university for a medical student to study. On 23 October 1934, the Prince of Wales dug out the first piece of turf and on 14 July 1938, the completed hospital began operating. The king and queen visited on 1 March 1939 and the queen proudly gave her name to the hospital – the Queen Elizabeth Hospital – often just referred to as the QE.

A WRITER AND AN MP

Barbara Cartland, the writer of 723 novels, was born in Edgbaston in 1901. Her father was a major in the British Army and her grandfather, James, was a brass manufacturer who ran James Cartland & Son Ltd. In 1918, her father was killed in action and her mother moved the family to London.

Fifteen years later, her brother, John Ronald Hamilton Cartland, returned to Birmingham as the Conservative Member for King's Norton. He won the seat in 1935. His speeches in Parliament often warned of the Nazi regime, having witnessed it himself when visiting Germany, and in 1937 he joined the Territorial Army. As war became imminent, he became a lieutenant in the Worcestershire and Oxford Yeomanry in August 1939. Sadly, he was killed in action on 30 May 1940. Even more tragic was the fact that his brother James had died the previous day.

His sister, Barbara had published her first book in 1923. Her last was published in 1997, three years before her death, then some of her unpublished manuscripts were published under the title 'The Pink Collection'.

A POPULAR DRINKING HOLE

Famous for its 'snob screens', the Bartons Arms opened in 1901 as the flagship for the Mitchell's & Butler's brewery of Cape Hill. Snob screens separated the middle classes from the working classes and although the middle classes could see the working classes, the working classes couldn't see them.

Sitting on the High Street in Aston, very close to the Aston Hippodrome, it saw many famous faces walk through its doors while appearing at that theatre. These included Laurel and Hardy, Marie Lloyd, Enrico Caruso and Charlie Chaplin, many of whom either just went in for a drink or lodged there overnight.

The Bartons Arms.

A FUTURE PRIME MINISTER WHO NEARLY WASN'T

David Lloyd George was well known for being against the Boer War and often received abuse for his beliefs. Even his wife and son were ridiculed and snubbed by their friends. But it was in Birmingham that he suffered his worst attack.

On 18 December 1901, he arrived in Birmingham to give an anti-war speech at the Town Hall. But the Brummies had too much respect for their own Joseph Chamberlain, who was Colonial Secretary in the Conservative Government. They greeted Lloyd George with chants of 'traitor!' and 'pro-Boer!' Some were even shouting for him to be lynched. Stepping in to break up the crowd, the police escorted the young Liberal radical away to safety disguised as a policeman.

THE CUP THAT CHEERS

John Sumner was born in 1856. His grandfather, William Sumner, had a grocery business in the Bull Ring and John eventually took over that business from his own father in the 1890s.

After a few years he decided he wanted to do something different. Instead of selling tea loose over the counter, he wanted to package it and give it a brand name. After buying thirty chests of tea to experiment with and spending £200 on advertising, Typhoo Tea was born in 1903. Advertised as 'the tea that doctor's recommend', he chose the name Typhoo because his sister drank tea to help with her digestion, and Typhoo was similar to the word 'doctor' in Chinese.

A well-known packet still seen in supermarkets today.

In 1929, the Typhoo Tea Factory was built on Bordesley Street, but when the company was taken over by Schweppes, it closed down in 1978. After being derelict for many years, new life is now being breathed into it by the BBC, who plan to open new studios there in 2026.

THE LAST OF HER KIND

In 1905 the youngest daughter of Richard Tapper Cadbury died. Emma Gibbons had been a well-known figure in Birmingham. In fact, she was the last of her kind, always dressed in the old Quaker costume.

A Quaker lady.

A YOUNG BOY WHO LOVED DRAWING

Herbert Austin was born in 1866 in Buckinghamshire, but the family moved to South Yorkshire, where his father worked as a farm bailiff. As a small boy he loved drawing, particularly anything mechanical, so on leaving school his parents thought he should take up architecture. However, Herbert was also interested in engineering.

In 1884, his uncle visited from Australia and when he returned home his nephew went with him. Herbert found himself a job in engineering and also found himself a wife. Nine years later, he returned to England, where he had been offered a directorship with the Wolseley Company, the same company he was working for in Australia.

The Sydney Works were based along Alma Street in Aston and named after the company's original birthplace. It was here that Herbert designed his first car, which he drove to Rhyl and back in June 1898. The Wolseley Autocar No. 1 averaged about 8 mph and so at a distance of 255 miles, that must have been quite a journey. The success of this three-wheeled car meant the four-wheeled Wolseley Voiturette appeared a year later.

In 1905, Herbert Austin decided to set up on his own and develop his own motorcar. He took on a young draughtsman, Albert Hancock, and turning a bedroom into an office, the designs for his new car developed. When looking for a permanent place, he discovered some empty workshops at Longbridge and with a small team, the first Austin car was built in readiness for the motor exhibition in November 1905.

Life for the young boy who loved drawing changed immensely during the rest of his life. In 1919, he was persuaded to stand as the Unionist Member for King's Norton and having won at the general election, he remained in Parliament until 1924. Then in 1936, he was given the title of Baron Austin of Longbridge.

A DISASTER IN THE MINE

The Hamstead Colliery had been established in 1875 on land on the Perry Hall estate and because of flooding, the mine had at one time the deepest shaft in the world. On 4 March 1908, thirty men went down at five o'clock to start their night shift. Twenty-six of those men didn't come out alive.

Not long after the start of the shift a fire broke out and the men were trapped. Rescue was impossible because the fire and smoke blocked off the entrances, so rescuers were unable to reach the trapped men. It took five days for the bodies to be lifted out of the mine.

At the inquest the men who had escaped told their stories. They worked with naked candles and one miner seems to have lit his candle too close to the box holding all the candles and a spark gradually ignited the box. The jury at the inquest recommended that candles should not be stored in the mine.

AN OLD OAK AND AN OLD FARMHOUSE

In May 1909, the oak tree that had given Selly Oak its name was chopped down. With the expansion of Selly Oak in the late 1800s, building work on the corner of Bristol Road and Oak Tree Lane had damaged its roots, causing it to become a stag oak. The stump was afterwards erected in Selly Oak Park as a memorial. Later, it underwent dendrochronology testing, which showed that it originated from around 1710.

A story was often told about how it had come to be. A local witch had been buried with an oak stake pierced through her heart and the stake had grown into a tree.

Also removed from Selly Oak around this time was an old farmhouse dating back to 1476 that, although not the manor house, had been given the name Selly Manor. In the 1800s, the surrounding land was developed and the house was divided into two cottages. It now needed renovation, and the suggestion was that it be demolished. However, George Cadbury came to its assistance. He arranged for it to be demolished, brick by brick, and rebuilt on the green in Bournville, where it is now a museum.

AN OLD PUB, A NEW SITE

The Golden Lion Inn had stood in Deritend, opposite the Old Crown, since the 1500s. It had been used as a Guild Hall, a tannery and then an inn, but in 1911 it was relocated to Cannon Hill Park to be used as a cricket pavilion.

A year later, it was set on fire by Suffragettes. Luckily, park staff noticed the flames and were able to put it out before any damage was done and it continued to be used as a cricket pavilion and tearoom until the early 1980s.

Unfortunately, around the late 1990s it was left abandoned due to structural issues, and it has since become derelict. However, in 2023 plans were being made to raise money to renovate it. This was estimated at about £40,000, but Historic England have pledged £32,000, so it is hoped this old building will be renovated.

A FATEFUL BUSINESS MEETING

In 1912, William Edward Hipkins was the Managing Director for W. & T. Avery Ltd at Soho and arrangements had been made for him to visit a new factory in Milwaukee. Born in Birmingham in 1857, William's family had their own business in Birmingham making various metal parts and fittings, which he had taken over from his father. But his skills in management soon came to the attention of others and in 1890 he was appointed managing director of John & Edwin Wrights, ropemakers. Then four years later, he joined the board at W.& T. Avery's and became their managing director in 1896.

It was Hipkins who had suggested opening a factory in America as a way of avoiding trade tariffs. No sooner had the factory opened than the company received a large order from the US Government. With an order like that, Hipkins had no hesitation in making the journey across the Atlantic to seal the deal in person. So, he booked a first-class ticket on the new unsinkable liner named RMS *Titanic*. His body was never found.

AN ACTOR'S LIFE

Barry Jackson was born in King's Norton in 1879, the son of a wealthy businessman. His parents loved the theatre, so from an early age he saw many theatrical performances, including his first Shakespeare play, *The Taming of the Shrew*, when he was just 10 years old. After travelling Europe for a couple of years, he came back to Birmingham and worked in an architect's office.

His love for the theatre resulted in him forming an amateur company in 1907 called the Pilgrim Players. They became so successful that four years later, they became a professional company. Jackson now felt they needed a permanent place to perform, so a small theatre in Station Street was built. With a capacity of 464 seats, it opened in 1913 with a performance of *Twelfth Night*. The Birmingham Repertory Theatre went on to become the starting point for many of our great actors, such as Laurence Olivier, Ralph Richardson and Edith Evans.

The Old Repertory Theatre.

TWO WARS AND IN BETWEEN

On 28 June 1914, the Austrian Archduke Franz Ferdinand was assassinated and this led to a chain of events that meant that on 4 August, Britain declared war on Germany. The men of Birmingham flocked to the recruiting stations and by the end of the first week, 4,500 had enlisted. Initially known as the 1st, 2nd and 3rd Birmingham Battalions, they were soon incorporated into the 14th, 15th and 16th Warwickshire Regiments.

Being so far inland, Birmingham saw little action, apart from all the men leaving to fight in foreign lands and many not returning, or returning as very different men. There were, however, three occasions when a Zeppelin managed to reach Birmingham, and during those three raids there was only one fatality, whose name was Jacko.

One night in October 1917, bombs were dropped over the Austin factory in Longbridge. Down the road was 'Manor House', in Northfield, the home of Dame Elizabeth Cadbury. A stray incendiary fell there, killing her pet monkey, Jacko.

Of course, there was war work, and during the war the Birmingham Small Arms Factory employed 20,000 workers who made 10,000 Lee–Enfield rifles each week and, over the four years of war, 145,397 Lewis guns.

A BIRMINGHAM SOLDIER TELLS THE CHRISTMAS STORY

Herbert Smart played for Aston Villa, but Christmas 1914 saw him in the trenches in Flanders. A gunner with the 5th Battery, Royal Field Artillery, he described that festive period when writing home, 'The Germans had a Christmas tree in the trenches and Chinese lanterns along the top of the parapet.'

He then told how they heard a German soldier calling to them and inviting them over. They didn't know what to do, but then one soldier decided to risk it. When nothing happened to him, the others decided to follow. When Herbert went, he exchanged some cigarettes for cigars.

One German soldier he met had been a waiter in London so could speak a little bit of English and told Herbert they didn't want to fight. The commanding officer had told them only three men could go at a time, but many soldiers met in no man's land that day, and as Herbert wrote, 'Fancy a German shaking your flapper as though he was trying to smash your fingers, and then a few days later trying to plug you! I hardly know what to think.'

THEY SHALL NOT GROW OLD

By the end of the war, 12,320 Birmingham men and women had been killed and 35,000 wounded. To commemorate them, the Hall of Memory was built. The foundation stone was laid on 12 June 1923 by the Prince of Wales. Costing £60,000 to erect and made of Portland Stone, it was unveiled by Prince Arthur of Connaught on 4 July 1925.

Sitting around the dome-like sarcophagus and placed on granite pedestals are four statues that represent the army, navy, air force and the women's services. Inside the hall, which is entered through large bronze doors, are the Books of Remembrance.

HOMES FIT FOR HEROES

Returning soldiers needed new homes for themselves and their families away from the slums they had lived in before the war. The first council houses were built in 1919 at Alum Rock and, over the ensuing years, thousands of new homes were built for the growing population. By 25 July 1930, 30,000 council houses had been built in Birmingham, and by 23 October 1933 there were 40,000. No. 30, Hopstone Road on the Weoley Castle estate, was officially opened by Neville Chamberlain as the 40,000th council house to be completed.

With Lea Hall, on 20 June 1939, the amount of council houses in Birmingham reached a total of 50,000. Over thirty-one new estates had been built, with the largest being Kingstanding, which covered 493 acres and held 4,802 houses.

JESSIE EDEN

The Representation of the People's Act was passed on 6 February 1918, which allowed women over the age of 30 to vote. It was a great victory for women's suffrage, although some women felt it was only a small step forward for women's rights.

Jessie Eden was just 16 years old when this Act was passed but by 1925, while working at the Joseph Lucas Motor Components Factory, she had become a shop steward for the Transport & General Workers' Union. This was a time when the working classes had had enough, and mass protests were a regular thing.

In 1926 the General Strike took place. At the Lucas factory, most of its women workers (around 10,000) didn't belong to a union, but undeterred, Jessie marched the women in her section out. She was later to tell her story on the fiftieth anniversary in 1976 how 25,000 people took part in the May Day March:

> One policeman put his hands on my arm. They were telling me to go home but the crowd howled leave her alone and then some men came and pushed the policemen away. They didn't do anything after that. I think they could see that there would have been a riot. I was never frightened of the police or the troops because I had the people with me.

Jessie didn't stop there. In 1931, Lucas adopted new working practices that saw female workers almost at the point of collapse. This time, Jessie took 10,000 women out on a seven-day strike. Following this, she became unpopular with her employers, so she spent the next two years in Moscow rallying Russian women.

By 1939, she was back in Birmingham and actively involved in the Birmingham Rent Strike, which saw 49,000 tenants go out in prostest. A popular public speaker, she continued her work well into the 1960s, and at the age of 67 she was leading protest marches against the Vietnam War.

REMOVED BRICK BY BRICK

In the 1920s, Hams Hall in Saltley stood derelict. Meanwhile, shipping magnate Oswald Harrison was searching for a house in Gloucestershire. So far, he had been unsuccessful in finding his ideal home. When he spotted Hams Hall, it was just what he was looking for – except it wasn't in the area he wanted.

Undaunted, he still bought it and had it transported, brick by brick, to Coates, near Cirencester, where it was rebuilt. After his death, now known as Bledisloe Lodge, it was taken over by the Royal Agricultural College and used as students' lodgings.

BIRMINGHAM'S BULL ON THE RAMPAGE

In 1927 there was panic in the Rag Market in Lower Smithfield. A cry was heard at the entrance of 'mad bull!' and the crowd of around 2,000–3,000 made a mad dash for the exits.

The bull was soon under control within seconds of it escaping. However, the panic-stricken crowd weren't. Women were screaming and children were being thrown into basket carriages for safety. And with only one policeman on duty, there was little he could do. In fact, he found himself almost crushed in the stampede of human feet, rather than those of the animal.

Word got round that the animal had been caught and the crowd became calmer. That is, until someone shouted that the beast was returning. Stalls were knocked over in the stampede, with broken crockery strewn everywhere. Purses were lost and children were separated from their mothers. Luckily, the injuries were minor and only eight women and one child had to be treated in hospital.

THE TRAGIC WEST END STAR

Fred Barnes was born in Saltley in 1885, the son of a butcher. He went on to find fame and fortune, only for his life to end in tragedy.

As a child, Fred was fascinated by the music hall and would hang around the stage door watching the artistes arrive. On one occasion, he saw Vesta Tilly arrive in her carriage and was captivated by her. He would later go on to call himself the male Vesta Tilly.

His first performance was at the Curzon Hall in November 1905, where he received good reviews. Various other appearances led to a sixteen-week season at Blackpool in 1906. He then came back to appear in pantomime at the Alexandra Theatre. From then on, his career blossomed and during the 1920s he was the toast of the West End. It was he who first popularised the songs 'On Mother Kelly's Doorstep' and 'Give Me The Moonlight, Give Me The Girl'.

But Fred had a secret, which in those days made life difficult for him. He was gay. Finding solace in alcohol, he began drinking heavily, even missing some of his performances, and soon he wasn't getting booked any more.

On 22 October 1938, he was found on his kitchen floor close to the gas oven. He had died of gas poisoning. But was it suicide? No one knows. Insufficient evidence meant the coroner gave an open verdict.

Fred was brought home to be buried in Saltley Churchyard.

NEW NAMES

As Birmingham spread out across the surrounding countryside, many new names appeared. One of these was for an area along Maypole Lane that grew up around the crossroads of King's Norton, Solihull and Alcester. You would think that Maypole was named for that – a place where country folk danced around a pole. But with the area being unpopulated before the nineteenth and early twentieth centuries, this is unlikely. However, being on a crossroads, where a pole would stand directing the coaches and carts, it is likely that this is how it got its name.

THE SHIRE IN BIRMINGHAM

In 1937 J.R.R. Tolkien published *The Hobbit*, a book in which Birmingham had been the inspiration for certain locations. Although he was not born in Birmingham, he had spent his early formative years there and had been educated at King Edward VI School.

Both his parents originated from the area. His father was from Handsworth and his mother Birmingham, but Tolkien had been born in South Africa in 1892, where his father was a banker. When he died in 1895, Tolkien's mother brought the family back to King's Heath, and after a short time they settled in Sarehole (Hall Green). When his mother died in 1904, he and his brother became the wards of their Catholic priest in Edgbaston.

When writing *The Hobbit* and *The Lord of the Rings*, his childhood memories of playing in and visiting parts of Birmingham were a great inspiration to him. As well as the village of Hall Green, these also included Birmingham University and 'Old Joe', Edgbaston Waterworks, Perrott's Folly, the Cole Valley and the smoky atmosphere of the industry on the edge of the Black Country.

A PIECE OF WHITE PAPER

Born in 1869, Neville Chamberlain was the youngest son of Joseph Chamberlain. Educated first at the Rugby School, he then went to Mason College, Birmingham. His studies over, he spent six years managing his father's plantation in the Bahamas before returning to Birmingham and working for Hoskins & Co., who made metal plates for shipping.

But politics was in his blood, and he became a councillor in 1911 and then Lord Mayor of Birmingham in 1915. Elected as MP for Ladywood in 1918, he refused to serve under Lloyd George's coalition government. But five years later, he was made Minister of Health. In 1931, he became Chancellor, and six years later he succeeded Stanley Baldwin as prime minister.

Following a meeting with Hitler in Munich in 1938, he came back waving his famous piece of white paper, announcing there would be 'peace in our time'. His optimism was short-lived and on 3 September 1939 he declared war against Germany. But it was always felt that he had brought Britain twelve months' reprieve, giving it time to prepare.

With the first few months of the war proving to be a disaster, and amid the fear that Germany would win, he resigned as prime minister on 10 May 1940. Six months later, he had died of bowel cancer.

PREPARATIONS FOR WAR

The fear of war had taken hold in 1935, so it was decided that ARP (Air Raid Precaution) leaflets were to be distributed to local councils. These circulars gave advice regarding training in anti-gas procedures and how to set up adequate emergency services. But even though the Birmingham Corporation formed a special committee, in these early days there was a certain amount of complacency.

Everyone had different ideas about what was best. Luckily, as war became more imminent, everything seemed to have fallen into place. A fortified basement in the Council House provided an office for the wartime controller, Sir Frank Wiltshire, who before the war had been the Town Clerk. He was appointed by the Home Office as Regional ARP Commissioner for the Midlands.

In August 1938, cellars and basement surveys were carried out. They were then classified and marked out for use. Trenches were dug in parks to act as shelters. Lined with concrete and steel, they were big enough to hold fifty people. The distribution of Anderson shelters began in February. They were free, but if people could afford it they were expected to make a donation.

Between February and November 1939, 100,000 shelters were delivered. They had to be erected in holes dug 4ft deep. The community spirit soon displayed itself as neighbours joined together and dug together in their respective gardens. Of course, you needed a garden to have an Anderson shelter, so people living in the old streets of the city centre and the old back-to-backs at first had to rely on the available cellars and public shelters. However, by 1941, Morrison shelters were being handed out. These were steel tables that could be erected inside the house. And where there was room, the council also started building brick shelters in the small yards around the back-to-backs.

To help prevent bombing and act as protection, certain measures began to appear, such as barrage balloons, with their distinctive cigar shape, which floated around the skies, the idea being that enemy aircraft would not be able to get too low over the city, making their attacks less accurate. Searchlights lit the night skies and the fire from anti-aircraft units ricocheted in all directions together with flares from other ack-ack units.

A LONG HOLIDAY FOR CHILDREN?

The evacuation of children from the inner cities was planned in detail. On the first day, children, together with a teacher, would leave the city. The second day was set aside for the younger children and mothers-to-be. To make sure everything ran smoothly, a test took place on 20 July 1939 from Hockley Station involving nine schools.

The 'at-risk' area was assessed and decided to be outward from the city centre to Aston in the north, Stirchley in the south, Handsworth in the west, and Saltley and Small Heath in the east. On 1 September 1939, the evacuation began for real, and the first train left at 8.20 a.m., followed by many others throughout that and the following day.

The children were taken to Evesham, Henley-in-Arden and other parts of Worcestershire and Warwickshire. Others went further afield to Gloucestershire and Herefordshire. Some went as far as South Wales. The families who accepted the evacuees were paid 9*s* per child.

Around 30,000 children were evacuated in the early stages of the war, together with 406 pregnant women, 4,135 mothers and 7,858 children under 5. There were also sixteen blind and four disabled adults. However, within a few days, 90 per cent of the young mothers returned, homesick and feeling isolated in the openness of the countryside. Once the air raids began another 22,000 children were evacuated.

SUSPICIOUS FOREIGNERS?

At the start of the war the British people were counted, and any foreigners were categorised. Some were sent immediately to internment camps. Others were restricted as to where they could go and what they could do.

As war progressed others were rounded up for the camps. In Birmingham, this included 100 women. Many worked as domestic servants and others were the innocent wives of Brummies who just happened to be either German or Italian.

THE AIR-RAID WARDEN

An Air-Raid Wardens' Service was set up consisting of both paid wardens and volunteers. The teams were divided into groups, working either day or night shifts. Their jobs were ensuring people kept to the black-out procedures, handing out gas masks and helping people fit them. During air raids they were to report for duty immediately, and they would direct people to their nearest air-raid shelter, assist in medical and rescue issues and generally help to keep people calm.

During heavy air raids fires needed to be put out, and these could be in the hundreds, so the regular fire service was supported by volunteers, the AFS (Auxiliary Fire Service). During the first few months of the war, 10,000 men and women volunteered to join the AFS.

THE REAL DAD'S ARMY

On 14 May 1940, a radio broadcast appealed for Local Defence Volunteers (known as the Home Guard). Recruitment took place at local police stations, and within a few days 30,000 men had volunteered. Set up to protect important factories and transport systems, the Home Guard also had to deal with any emergencies or an enemy landing by parachute. Some factories formed their own Home Guard.

With no uniform to begin with, they paraded in their own clothes and carried brooms for their arms drill. Eventually, they received denim overalls and badges, before receiving an actual uniform that consisted of a serge battledress. Early in 1941 they got their rifles, and in July they took part in an exercise to practise defending Birmingham from invasion, which proved 100 per cent successful.

INDUSTRY LEARNS TO ADAPT

Being a town of industry, Birmingham found the transition from peacetime manufacturing to war work quick and easy and was soon up in second place behind London in its production of war material. The largest purpose-built factory was in Castle Bromwich. Called the Castle Bromwich Aeroplane Factory, it produced 100 Supermarine Spitfires and twenty Avro Lancaster bombers per month during the war. By the end of the war, around 12,000 spitfires and 305 Lancasters had been produced there.

The BSA (Birmingham Small Arms) Company began a seven-day working week to supply the armed forces with rifles and machine guns, as well as arms for Spitfires and Hurricanes. Fourteen other factories were requisitioned, and a new factory was built in Kitt's Green. At its peak during the war, the BSA had control of sixty-seven factories employing 28,000 workers.

On 19 November 1941, two direct hits during a raid destroyed the southern end of the factory. Fifty-three workers were killed and eighty-nine injured. Two months later, the original gun-makers' building took a hit, but luckily the workers had evacuated.

Shadow factories, so named because they operated in the 'shadow' of existing motor companies to conceal their true purpose and protect them from becoming targets, produced engines and aircraft. Rover built two, one in South Yardley and the other in Solihull. They made parts for Bristol Hercules engines. Austin extended its own factory to produce aircraft and became known as Austin Aero. Morris built a shadow factory in Castle Bromwich and produced Spitfires and Lancasters. And in these newly built factories, the 15,000 workers were protected by purpose-built underground tunnels.

Many other Birmingham factories turned out for the war effort and all sorts of bits and pieces were made at factories that were equipped to do so. Fort Dunlop in Erdington made tyres for army vehicles and experimented with bulletproof tyres. Radiators and air coolants for Spitfires and Hurricanes were made by Serck Radiators in Greet and the Joseph Lucas factory in Hockley made numerous parts for aeroplanes. Even jewellers switched to making intricate parts for various components.

By the end of the war, about 400,000 workers had all somehow contributed and done their bit for the war effort.

FOOTBALL TAKES A BACK SEAT

At the start of the 1939–40 football season, it was decided by the directors at Aston Villa not to take part in any of the national or local competitions. The ground had been taken over for more important things. A similar situation prevented them from using their alternative ground, so they had no choice but to suspend their involvement in competitions. Anyone visiting the ground, instead of seeing men running around with a ball would see sheep happily grazing on the pitch.

KEEPING THE WINDOWS SAFE

Edward Burne-Jones had been born in Birmingham in 1833 and quickly showed a talent for artistry. He became a painter and created many stained-glass windows, but the best were considered to be those he created for St Philip's. The four large stained-glass windows had been commissioned between 1885 and 1891 and were considered so special that they were removed by the Birmingham Civic Society at the beginning of the war and kept stored inside a slate mine in Wales.

BOMBS AND MORE BOMBS

Between 9 August 1940 and 23 April 1943, Birmingham was constantly being bombed, with the worst raids taking place between August 1940 and April 1941. During those years, there were seventy-seven air raids, in which 2,241 were killed and 3,010 seriously injured. And the damage amounted to 140,336 houses, 4,003 offices and 654 public buildings either being damaged or destroyed.

The tower and portico are all that remain of St Thomas' Church.

And the worst night was 19–20 November 1940. That night, no anti-aircraft guns were in action as it had been chosen for an experiment for Hampden aircraft to practise night interception. The experiment was a success, but at the expense of the people of Birmingham.

Those killed in the Blitz are remembered in the Peace Garden in the grounds of St Thomas' Church. All that is left of this church is its bell tower. It too was a casualty of the war, being hit by bombs at 7.25 p.m. on 11 December 1940 and destroyed.

A POPULAR TRAIN BORN IN BIRMINGHAM

Between 1940 and 1946, Wilbert Awdry was curate of St Nicolas' Church in King's Norton. During his time there, he started writing stories to amuse his son, Christopher, who was suffering with measles. At first, he thought of telling stories about tanks. But other stories had been in his head for some time.

As a small boy, he listened to the trains running along a track near his home and so the characters of his stories became trains. The first book in 'The Railway Series' was published in 1945. He went on to write another twenty-six books, the last in 1972. Later Christopher wrote another sixteen between 1983 and 2011.

The books made a star out of one of the characters. In 1984, Thomas the Tank Engine was given his own television series called *Thomas & Friends*. The series ran until 2021, but repeats will probably still be seen by children for many years to come.

REBUILDING BIRMINGHAM

Birmingham was in ruins but the Brummies weren't downhearted. Their city would be rebuilt. Their industries would go on and shattered lives would be mended. Birmingham would be bigger and better than it was before, there was no doubt about that. After the First World War, Birmingham had become known as the second city, so the second city was going to show the world what it was made of. And to do that it needed help.

FROM FOREIGN LANDS

On 21 June 1948, HMT *Empire Windrush* arrived at Tilbury Docks. The following day, passengers disembarked. A new community had arrived in England from the Caribbean, invited by the Colonial Office to help rebuild Britain following the British Nationality Act 1948. Known as the Windrush Generation, many of them found their way to Birmingham.

They may have been invited by the Colonial Office, but they unfortunately weren't always welcomed by the people of Birmingham. However, they built their communities and have become Brummies, just as the Saxons and then the Normans did many years ago. They have contributed to Birmingham's culture with their music and art and have given the city a multicultural element. An example of this is UB40. A band of mixed races with music that captures the reggae rhythm of the Caribbean. Then there was poet Benjamin Zephaniah, who brought a touch of Jamaica to his words.

TELEVISION COMES TO BIRMINGHAM

The Gosta Green Studios opened in 1956 using the Alexandra Repertory Company to produce a half-hour play called *Story Conference*. Others followed, and three years later, more adventurous productions were made when the six-part adaptation of Arnold Bennett's *Hilda Lessways* was broadcast, with the title role being played by Judi Dench.

These first productions were all broadcast live. It wasn't until 1960 that pre-recorded dramas were made. Production continued throughout the 1960s until the new Pebble Mill Studios were opened in 1971. Here, for the next thirty years, many popular dramas and series were produced.

Also arriving in Birmingham in 1956 was the ATV independent channel. The studios here also produced many favourites: variety shows with big stars such as Tom Jones and Engelbert Humperdinck; quiz shows like *The Golden Shot* and *Bullseye*; and Birmingham's attempt to take on soap opera land's favourite *Coronation Street* with its own *Crossroads*.

THE STREET IN THE SKY

The late 1950s saw a new style of dwelling for the people of Birmingham. Like the court-style buildings of the nineteenth century, they were designed to house as many people as possible. They were, of course, the high-rise flats. What a joy for the people of the old damp and dirty homes that the back-to-backs had become, to move into these multistorey buildings, all with modern amenities.

The first of these was built in Duddeston in 1959. Advertised as giving superb views over the city, the people were told it was a new type of community life. They would be able to chat to their neighbours on the landings of the building and there would be children's play areas. It would be an ideal way of living.

It was at first, but with the rapidly increasing demand for housing during the following decade, corners were cut in regard to the building of the blocks. By the 1980s and 1990s they were not so desirable. Leaky roofs, damp in the walls and the bright white concrete being turned grey by pollution were the least of the problems. Long, narrow corridors, dark corners and secluded doorways led to crime and antisocial behaviour.

AN OLD FIRM HELPS OUT

The 1950s and 1960s saw Birmingham develop quickly following the bomb damage of the war. One company, which had been in existence since the 1880s, was to benefit from this.

Walter Frederick Bannock had set up his marble, granite and slate business in the 1880s in Stone Yard, Deritend. By the 1950s the company was based in Hall Green. They supplied the marble cladding used to smarten up the façades of hotels, banks, office blocks and even the Bull Ring Shopping Centre.

AN OLD MAN'S FANTASY?

Was a 60-year-old mystery solved in 1958 or was it just a story told by an old man?

Henry James Burge was 80 years old (although conflicting reports suggest he was 75) and after a lifetime of crime – forty-seven years in total were spent in prison for various petty crimes – he was now living in a nursing home. He told his tale to a newspaper, the *Sunday Pictorial*, which appeared in the 23 February 1958 edition. They even published a photograph of Henry showing how he forced open the door of the shop he burgled.

So, what was the mystery object he had supposedly stolen? It was the English Cup, later to be known as the FA Cup, which was never seen again after the theft.

In 1895, Aston Villa won the cup in the final against West Bromwich Albion at Crystal Palace, winning 1–0. The fans were naturally over the moon, so the cup was displayed in the small sports shop of William Shillcock in Aston for all to see. The shop was basically the front room of a house in Newtown Row, where William was well known for making football boots and balls. But on the night of 11 September, someone broke in and stole the cup. Despite extensive police investigations, it was never found.

Henry said that now he was an old man he wanted to get things off his chest, and he confessed to being involved in the robbery. He said that he and two other men had broken open a back door with a crowbar and the silver trophy had been melted down the same night and made into fake coins. He said they also stole some football boots.

However, there was a discrepancy to his story. Reports at the time stated that the robbers had got in through the roof, not the back door. Mr Shillcock had arrived at his shop in the morning to find plaster on the floor and, looking up, had seen a hole in the roof. The thieves had stolen some coins from the till but no football boots were said to be missing.

A NEW SHOPPING CENTRE

The Bull Ring has been part of Birmingham's shopping experience since the twelfth century, when an open market was held around St Martin's Church. It was also the place where bull baiting took place, hence the name – Bull Ring. Then came Mercer Street with its growing cloth trade. Later, it became known as Spicer Street, then Spiceal Street, due to all the butchers and grocers. But now a new type of shop filled the area.

In 1961, work began on the new Bull Ring Shopping Centre, which was opened by Prince Philip on 26 May 1964. It had both an outdoor market and an indoor area filled with many different sorts of shops.

The Bull Ring as it was.

The new Bull Ring Shopping Centre.

It was very popular and retail outlets in other parts of Birmingham complained they were losing business. But the building didn't last. Made of concrete, which was common practice in the 1960s, it had begun to look very weather-worn by the 1980s. So, plans were made to replace it and the new building opened in 2003.

A NEW ARTS CENTRE

John English and his wife Mollie loved the theatre. In 1948, they set up the Arena Theatre Company and entertained the people of the Birmingham area in town halls in the winter and outside in parks in the summer. Every summer between 1949 and 1961, they performed in Cannon Hill Park.

Councillor Sir Frank Price wanted to do two things – make the arts more accessible to local communities and improve Birmingham's landscape. So, joining forces, the three enthusiasts created the Midland's Art Centre (MAC), which opened in Cannon Hill Park in 1962. The MAC offered a varied programme from plays to films, art exhibitions, craft fairs and courses.

THE BIRMINGHAM SCENE

In the 1960s, for followers of pop music Liverpool was the place to be, The Beatles had made sure of that. But Birmingham was soon answering back.

The first to take on Liverpool were The Rockin' Berries, who had formed while at Turves Green School in the 1950s. Originally named because they played numerous Chuck Berry songs, they had their first hit, 'He's in Town', in 1964.

In 1963, two brothers from Great Barr, Steve and Muff Winwood, joined up with Spencer Davis and Pete York to form The Spencer Davis Group and had their first hit in 1965. Two years later, Steve went on to form the more progressive rock group Traffic.

Meanwhile, local lad Roy Wood from Kitts Green was making his mark. In the early 1960s he formed a band called The Falcons. Then, after appearing with a couple of other bands, he formed The Move and their first single, 'Night of Fear', soared to No. 2 in the charts in 1967. A few months later, their third single, 'Flowers in the Rain', was the first song played on the new BBC radio station Radio 1. Later, Roy formed the Electric Light Orchestra with Jeff Lyne (a Shard End local who later co-founded The Travelling Wilburys) and in 1972 went on to have more success in a band called Wizzard.

One of the members of The Move and ELO was Bev Bevan. Born in South Yardley in 1944, he had been in a couple of bands before The Move – The Diplomats, with Denny Laine, and The Vikings, with Carl Wayne, both musicians born in Birmingham. When Roy Wood left ELO, Bevan remained with them for many years before forming his own band, The Bev Bevan Band.

In May 1964, Denny Laine joined forces with Mike Pinder from Erdington to form The Moody Blues and within a few months had moved to London to find fame and fortune. Meanwhile, Carl Wayne was the lead singer with The Move and when they disbanded, he began a solo career, then in the 1990s took to the stage in musical theatre, appearing in *Blood Brothers*.

The first time 14-year-old John Michael Osborne heard The Beatles singing 'She Loves You', he knew exactly what he wanted to be. John was born in 1948 and grew up in Aston. In 1967, he joined the band Rare Breed as their singer but two years later, he joined fellow Brummies, Terence 'Geezer' Butler, Bill Ward and Tony Iommi, the son of Italian immigrants, to form a group. They took the name Black Sabbath and Ozzy's wish came true.

A bench celebrating Black Sabbath on the bridge in Broad Street.

NEW ROADS AND AN ITALIAN DISH

In the 1960s, part of Britain's development following the war was a network of new main roads and motorways. Many roads led to Birmingham, so in 1965, plans for an interchange at Gravelly Hill were unveiled that would connect many of them around Birmingham.

Construction began in 1968, and on 24 May 1972 Gravelly Hill Interchange was opened by Peter Walker, the Secretary of State for the Environment. It consisted of 13,000 tons of steel and 170,000 cubic yards of concrete, was supported by 559 concrete columns and had cost £10 million to build. To make room for it, a block of flats, 160 houses, a bank and a pub called the Erdington Arms had been demolished.

When a *Birmingham Mail* journalist first saw the plans, he referred to it as being similar to a plate of spaghetti. The name stuck, and the interchange has been known as Spaghetti Junction ever since.

A NIGHT THAT SHOOK THE CITY

The night of 21 November 1974 started as a normal one, with the pubs filling up with people who were out for a relaxing drink after a busy day or out with friends, catching up on what had happened since they'd last met. Boys out with girls, perhaps on a first date, and everyone enjoying themselves. But then, loud bangs echoed through two of those pubs, the Mulberry Bush and the Tavern in the Town. The IRA had struck again and this time in Birmingham.

As the smoke cleared and rescuers reached them, twenty-one people had been killed and more than 180 injured, making this the worst terrorist attack on mainland Britain by the IRA. The police immediately got to work and quickly made arrests. But had the police got it right?

The Birmingham Six, as they became known, were six Irishmen who were convicted in August 1975. Five had been arrested on the night of bombings as they were travelling back to Belfast. The sixth was arrested the next day. It all seemed cut and dried – forensic tests showed they had been handling explosives and four of them also signed statements admitting their involvement. But at the trial they protested their innocence, saying they had been mistreated and threatened while under arrest. Despite these allegations, they were all convicted in August 1975 and sentenced to life imprisonment.

Following appeals, a 1985 TV investigative programme showed that the test for evidence of explosives on the skin would be positive even if someone had just been smoking. Police also originally thought the bombs had been left in plastic bags, which the four had agreed, but it was now discovered that they had been in holdalls. Witnesses also testified that police had shown brutality in getting the confessions, but the appeal judges refused to believe the police would do such a thing.

Further investigative programmes were aired and eventually, in March 1991, a second appeal took place and this time the sentences were squashed. Whoever did plant those bombs has never been found.

A SPICY NEW DISH FOR THE ENGLISH PALATE

In the mid-1970s, a new dish was introduced in Birmingham. The introduction of exotic food from Asia dates back to 1945, when John's Restaurant, which eventually became known as The Darjeeling, opened at No. 122 Steelhouse Lane.

The Second World War had brought workers known as Lascars to our shores. They were cooks, who worked on merchant ships, and many found their way to Birmingham, where they worked as kitchen porters or cooks. Soon, some were opening their own restaurants, and by the 1950s there were The Koh I Noor on the Bristol Road, The Shah Bagh on Horsefair and The Jinnah in Balsall Heath.

The Jinnah was the first to introduce takeaway food. To overcome restrictions in their religious faiths about the supplying of alcohol, they introduced the 'bring your own' system. And their different opening hours also meant they were the only places open after the pubs had shut. So, the popular phrase 'going for a curry' after a night out was regularly heard.

The most popular dish in the 1970s was Chicken Tikka Masala, which had been created especially for British tastebuds, but other items on the menu soon became popular, such as Korma, Madras, Rogan Josh, Jalfrezi and Vindaloo. Then came the Balti, which was introduced in 1977 by a Pakistani restaurant in Balsall Heath, once again as something unique for the British tastebuds. Other restaurants began offering this dish around the Balsall Heath, Sparkhill and Sparkbrook district, quickly giving this area the name of the Balti Triangle.

BIRMINGHAM'S ANSWER TO BILLY CONNELLY

Robert Davis was born in Acocks Green in 1945 and was a school friend of Bev Bevan, both attending Moseley Grammar School. He, too, started a career in music but chose folk music rather than pop or rock. In between songs he would tell jokes and soon realised he had a gift for comedy. (Although he did have a hit record in August 1975, with a novelty song entitled 'Funky Moped'.) So, Jasper Carrott was born and his joke telling became monologues describing his observations of life and places he had visited. Old friends remain old friends, and today his shows usually include The Bev Bevan Band.

FROM REGGAE TO ROMANTICS

On 9 February 1979, a new band performed at the Hare and Hounds pub in King's Heath. The group of friends from Birmingham, from both white and West Indian backgrounds, who played a mixture of pop and reggae, had been jamming together for a while and had agreed to play for a friend's birthday party. After that, they continued to play in various pubs until they were spotted by Chrissie Hynde, who booked them to support her band, The Pretenders.

UB40 took their name from the card given to those who were claiming unemployment benefit and their first album in August 1980, which had been recorded in a bedsit in Birmingham, was entitled *Signing Off*, suggesting any claims for unemployment benefit were ending. It spent seventy-one weeks in the album charts.

Throughout the 1980s they enjoyed numerous hits in the singles charts and many live performances, but today, a split between the two brothers of the band, Ali and Robin Campbell, means there are two bands performing the old hits of the 1980s and 1990s.

Also starting out at the same time were three Birmingham lads, Stephen Duffy, Nick Rhodes and John Taylor, who formed a band while at college. Their first gig was at the Birmingham Polytechnic on 5 April 1979. They called themselves Duran Duran, after Dr Durand-Durand from the film *Barbarella* and it was only a couple of months later that they performed at the nightclub Barbarella's in Birmingham.

Not long after, Stephen Duffy left and was replaced by Roger Taylor, from Castle Bromwich. Later, two other members joined from other parts of the country, Simon Le Bon and Andy Taylor, and by 1984, their popularity was said to be rivalling the Beatlemania of the 1960s.

A PLACE TO BE SEEN

In the 1980s the place to be seen was the Rum Runner. Two brothers, Paul and Michael Berrow, wanted to provide the young people of Birmingham with somewhere different to go. Their family already owned a nightclub on Broad Street called the Rum Runner. It had been opened in 1964 by the previous generation of siblings, Don, Ray, Peter, Terrence and Georgina, together with licensee Tony Hurley, who had given £6,500 each to open a club.

In the 1970s Paul and Michael visited the well-known Studio 54 while in New York and wanted to bring a similar experience to Birmingham, so revamping the Rum Runner, it became the city's foremost discotheque. Later, it was here that Duran Duran had their big break. After playing at Barbarella's, they gave the Berrow brothers a demo tape. Impressed by what they heard, the brothers offered Duran Duran the use of their club for rehearsals and gigs.

But would the previous generation have approved? Don Berrow, during an interview in 2013, said he wouldn't have let the group in. They weren't smart enough for the club he had originally started. He even regularly refused Ozzy Osbourne and Bev Bevan entry to his club because they weren't smart enough. But he did allow frequent visitors Tommy Cooper and George Best in.

LITTLE CAR IN A BIG TOWN

Thomas the Tank Engine was not the only little vehicle to be born in Birmingham. In the 1990s, a little car also stole the hearts of children too.

First shown in 1991, it told of a little vintage car called Brum. Filmed around Birmingham, which in the stories is called Big Town, it was narrated by Birmingham's own Toyah Willcox, the King's Heath-born pop star turned actress. She also provided the voice of Brum. Each episode started with

Brum escaping from the Motor Museum to go on an adventure in Big Town. There were sixty-six stories told over four series between 1991 and 2001.

THE CANALS ONCE AGAIN COME ALIVE

All commercial traffic on Birmingham's canals had ceased by 1980. Once a hive of activity and crucial to the industries of the city, the canals had begun to decline as the railways took over, and then the roads and motorways. By the late 1980s they were in a state of disrepair, and it was realised they were becoming an eyesore.

A restoration programme was undertaken and soon new developments appeared – the International Convention Centre and the National Indoor Arena. Where warehouses and wharfs once stood is now one of the most popular areas in Birmingham.

Brindleyplace is home to bars and restaurants, cafés and shops plus an art gallery, sealife centre and theatre. Building began in 1993 with the first phase opening in 1995. The site was then completed in 2010.

Close to Brindleyplace is The Mailbox, which opened in 2000. Originally built in 1970 as the sorting office for Birmingham's post, it was the largest building in the city at the time. Before that the area was a railway goods yard connecting the railways and canals. It is now a large complex, which is not only home to numerous shops, restaurants and bars and offices, it is also home to the BBC after they moved from their Pebble Mill studios.

MODERN TIMES

With all the new renovations taking place in Birmingham, statues celebrating the past and looking to the future were unveiled over a period of time. The Forward Statue, made of polyester resin and erected in Centenary Square, represented Birmingham marching out of the industrial revolution and into modern times. It was a mixture of numerous figures, which included Joseph Chamberlain and Josiah Mason, plus imaginary characters blowing kisses to the past. Unfortunately, it was damaged by fire in 2003 and had to be removed.

'The Carpet Salesmen' all in gold.

Another, standing in Broad Street, depicts the larger-than-life figures of Boulton, Watt and Murdoch. Made of bronze with a gold coating and standing on a Portland stone plinth, the statue has been nicknamed both 'The Golden Boys' and 'The Carpet Salesmen' – the latter due to the large document being studied by the figures that resembles a piece of carpet.

A large fountain was erected in 1993 when Victoria Square was pedestrianised. Known as 'The River', it is one of the largest in Europe. Sitting in the upper section is a large female figure, who was supposed to represent the force of life. However, she soon became known as 'The Floozie in the Jacuzzi'.

But the most controversial of all stands outside the Library of Birmingham in Centenary Square. Called 'A Real Birmingham Family', it shows two Birmingham sisters, both single mothers, with their two children. One sister was pregnant when she modelled for the statue. Three hundred and fifty families were interviewed before the sisters were chosen. However, there was an outcry as many people felt the statue should be of a traditional father and mother with their children.

HOW THEY LIVED

In 2002 George Saunders moved out of his home and shop and left behind a legacy for future generations. He wasn't anyone out of the ordinary but what he left behind was. He was a tailor, who had come to Birmingham from St Kitts in 1958 and moved to Court 15 on Hinge Street and Hurst Street in 1974. Court 15 had been built in 1831 and in 2001 it was taken over by the National Trust. Each house in the court depicts a different era and a different family, with research having been undertaken to use examples of the actual people who lived in this court.

There were the Levys in 1851. Lawrence Levy and his sons, Joseph and Emmanuel, were watchmakers who had come to Birmingham from London to work. Then in the 1870s there

The narrow court-style back-to-backs that were home to so many families.

was the Oldfield family. Herbert was a glassmaker, and his wife Ann gave birth to ten children. And standing in their small home it is hard to imagine how this family all fitted in.

The Mitchell family had lived at Court 15, House 3 for 100 years by the 1930s, which was extremely unusual. George Mitchell had been born there in 1860, but his parents had moved there in 1840.

While places such as this (Court 15, Soho House and Aston Hall, among others) exist and are open to the public, the history of Birmingham will not be forgotten.

RESTORATION AND THE BBC

The Saracen's Head in King's Norton was built in 1492 and belonged to a wool merchant. It eventually became the Saracen's Head Inn. An exact date for this is not known. The first reference to it being an inn is in 1806, but it is possible that when a family named Lea acquired it in 1771, they may have turned it into an inn then. In the twentieth century, it was owned by Mitchell & Butler.

The Old Grammar School in King's Norton was built around 1434 and stands in St Nicolas' Churchyard. It is thought to have originally been the priest's house until it became the school. By the mid-twentieth century, both buildings had been given to St Nicolas' Church, but as the years went by, they were difficult

The Old Grammar School, King's Norton.

to keep in good repair and gradually became derelict. The parish realised it was going to be difficult to renovate them, so in 2004 they entered a competition.

It was for the BBC2 programme *Restoration*. Twenty-one properties took part in the competition, with eight being shortlisted, and the two King's Norton properties became the winners. They were pledged £2.5 million from the Heritage Lottery Fund. The restoration took four years and, when completed, the two buildings became known as Saint Nicolas' Place.

STONE AGE BRUMMIE REAPPEARS

In 2009, Birmingham had a visitor from the past, or rather evidence of their existence. Excavations for a new campus for Birmingham University revealed that Stone Age humans lived in Digbeth. Two flint tools that had been used to hunt with and cut food were found near Curzon Street. The team from Leicester University who were carrying out the work dated them back 10,400 years to the Mesolithic, or Middle Stone Age. There was also evidence of a layer of charcoal, showing that Stone Age humans had burned woodland to make clearings to build settlements. And fossilised pollen showed the area contained mosses with birch and pine trees.

FIVE YEARS IN THE MAKING

On 21 December 2017, Birmingham was in a state of excitement. It was announced that the 22nd Commonwealth Games would be held in the city in 2022.

The organising committee based themselves in Brindley Place and prepared for five years of planning, building and recruiting. First, a fee of £25 million had to paid to the Commonwealth Games Federation for the rights to hold the games, but the hope was that with the numerous visitors coming into Birmingham to enjoy all the events, the games would bring revenue back into the city.

Perry Barr was chosen as the main centre for the games as it already had the Alexandra Stadium, which would be totally revamped. Work also began in erecting new buildings, in particular the athletes' village, and revamping other buildings and improving the roads around Perry Barr. However, things didn't go as planned. Three years into the work, the whole country was hit by Covid, and things came to a standstill. The athletes' village didn't get finished in time and the athletes had to be housed in student accommodation. When the village was finally completed in April 2023, the apartments were put on the general market. However, a year later many were still empty.

But Birmingham was undeterred – the city would still put on a good show despite Covid. As the time approached for the games to take place, there was still a concern about the spread of the disease. A clinic would be set up to test all the competitors on their arrival and an isolation facility would also be available. And visitors were asked to wear masks when watching indoor events and to be very mindful of any symptoms they developed.

Seventy-two nations took part with 6,500 athletes partaking in 280 events throughout twenty different sports. And although the stars of the show were the athletes, all the volunteers came a close second. Fourteen months before the games began, volunteers were called for and 21,000 people were interviewed. Eventually, 14,000 went through a vigorous training programme and were given various jobs to do. They were continually praised by both the public and the press for all their hard work and enthusiasm.

The games were opened by King Charles III (then Prince of Wales) and the opening ceremony gave a vibrant example of Birmingham's history, showing routines depicting its industry and way of life. And, as a testament to Birmingham's old iron industry, it introduced a large metal bull, who stole the hearts

Following his appearance in the opening ceremony, the bull, made of nuts, bolts, chains and cogs, stood in Centenary Square for the duration of the Commonwealth Games, where he was visited by an estimated 4 million people.

of the spectators and now, having been given the name Ozzy, it lives in Central Station – the new, revamped version of New Street Station.

Although the games were a success, the preparations did cripple Birmingham financially and within twelve months the city was declared bankrupt. But then Joseph Chamberlain overspent with his vision of a new Birmingham too, so hopefully Birmingham will once again bounce back.

ANOTHER NEW TRAIN

It was way back in 2009 that the idea of a high-speed railway linking London with Birmingham, Manchester and Leeds was first mentioned. The first high-speed line ran from St Pancras in London through the Channel Tunnel to France, Belgium and the Netherlands. This is known as HS1, so the new line became known as HS2. Work began in 2017, but more recently it has been announced that the line will now stop in Birmingham and not continue to Manchester or Leeds.

The station in Birmingham is being built in Curzon Street and prior to the work starting, archaeological surveys took place. One of Birmingham's original stations was built here in the 1830s and the remains of this old station were found, which included a piece of apparatus designed by Robert Stephenson that has now received the accolade of being the oldest surviving piece of railway architecture.

When the railways first began, the London & North Western Railway took a chunk out of the Park Street burial ground. Now with HS2 doing the same, archaeologists have undertaken a twelve-month excavation of the area. They found 6,500 skeletons and evidence showed that some had been dissected after death by students of the medical school. Objects, such as lumps of coal, stones, even bricks, seemed to have been placed where organs would have been situated. Some had ornaments and jewellery buried with them – a custom that was often carried out in Victorian times. After all the skeletons have been removed, analysed and an attempt made to name them through records, they will be reburied in consecrated ground.

Today, as HS2 develops and we watch as the landscape is dramatically changed, we look back to the days of all the other changes Brummies have witnessed. And wonder, as we become part of history, what will future Brummies think of the changes we have made.

BIBLIOGRAPHY

Abbott, Eric George, *Old Birmingham: Work and Leisure* (Stenlake Publishing, 2002).

Alexander, Helen, *Richard Cadbury of Birmingham* (Hodder and Stoughton, 1906).

Anderton, Thomas, *A Tale of One City: The New Birmingham* (Midland Counties Herald Office, 1900).

Andrews, Eliezer, *John Skirrow Wright M.P.* (Cornish Brothers, Beacon & Nutt, and White, Birmingham, 1880).

Benton, Josiah H., *John Baskerville, Type-Founder and Printer, 1706–1775* (The Merrymount Press, 1914).

Bird, Vivian, *Portrait of Birmingham* (Hale, London, 1970).

Cattell, John, & Bob Hawkins, *The Birmingham Jewellery Quarter* (English Heritage, 2000).

Chinn, Carl, *Brum Undaunted: Birmingham During the Blitz* (Birmingham Library Services, 1996).

Chinn, Carl, *The Life of William Hutton* (Brewin Books, 1998).

Cornish, James, *Stranger's Guide Through Birmingham* (Cornish Brothers, 1851).

Davidson, Alfred, *A History of the Holtes of Aston* (E. Everitt, 1854).

Dent, Robert K., *Old and New Birmingham* (Houghton and Hammond, 1880).

Dent, Robert K., *The Making of Birmingham* (J.L. Allday, 1894).

Dugdale, William, *The Antiquities of Warwickshire* (J. Osborn & T. Longman, 1730).

Edwards, E., *Personal Recollections of Birmingham Men* (Midland Educational Trading Co. Ltd, 1877).

Foster, Andy, *Birmingham* (Buildings Books Trust, 2005).

Galton, Francis, *Memories of My Life* (Methuen & Co., 1908).

Hemingway, John, *Medieval Birmingham: People & Places, 1070–1553* (Archaeopress Publishing Ltd, 2022).

Hodder, Michael, *Birmingham: The Hidden History* (The History Press, 2004).

Hutton, William, *A History of Birmingham, 6th Edition. With Considerable Additions* (James Guest, 1836).

Langford, John Alfred, *A Century of Birmingham Life* (W.G. Moore & Co., 1871).
Masterman, J.H.B., *The Story of English Towns: Birmingham* (Society for Promoting Christian Knowledge, 1920).
Muirhead, J.H., *Nine Famous Birmingham Men* (Cornish Brothers Ltd, 1909).
Munro, Andy, *Going for a Balti* (Brewin Books, 2015).
Pye, Charles, *Description of Modern Birmingham* (J.M. Richardson, 1818).
Richardson, Amy, *Looking at Birmingham* (Brewin Books, 1994).
Ross, Mandy, *Children's History of Birmingham* (Hometown World, 2011).
Showell, Walter, & Thomas Harman, *Showell's Directory of Birmingham* (Cornish Brothers, 1885).
Skipp, Victor, *The Making of Victorian Birmingham* (V. Skipp, 1983).
Smith, Joshua Toulmin, *Memorials of Old Birmingham* (H. Wright, 1863).
Stephens, W.B., *A History of the County of Warwick, Vol. 17: The City of Birmingham* (Victoria County History, 1964).
Stowe, Charles, *The Life of Harriet Beecher Stowe: Her Letters and Journals* (Houghton, Mifflin & Company, 1891).
Upton, Dr Chris, *Back to Backs* (The National Trust, 2004).

UNCREDITED MAGAZINES AND PAMPHLETS

The Birmingham Town Hall, 1834–1934 (published for the General Purposes Committee by the City of Birmingham Information Bureau, 1934).
The Bournville Works Magazine (Cadbury Brothers Ltd, December 1955).
'Elizabeth Mary Cadbury', Memorial Number of the *Bournville Works Magazine* (Cadbury Brothers Ltd, 1952).
'Royal Visits to Bournville', Souvenir Number of the *Bournville Works Magazine* (Cadbury Brothers Ltd, 1939).

WEB PAGES (ACCESSED BETWEEN JANUARY AND APRIL 2024)

ancestry.co.uk
billdargue.jimdofree.com
birmingham.gov.uk
birminghamforum.co.uk
birminghamgems.com
birminghamhistory.net
birminghammail.co.uk
birminghammuseums.org.uk/resources/birmingham-windrush-generation
britannica.com
britishnewspaperarchive.co.uk
chamberlainhighburytrust.co.uk
findmypast.co.uk
fkwc.org
historywm.com
macearchive.org
mappingbirmingham.blogspot.com (A Tour of Lost Birmingham, Jen Dixon)
parliament.uk
revolutionaryplayers.org.uk
spartacus-educational.com
visitbirmingham.com
warwickshirerailways.com
windrush75.org
ww2talk.com

INDEX